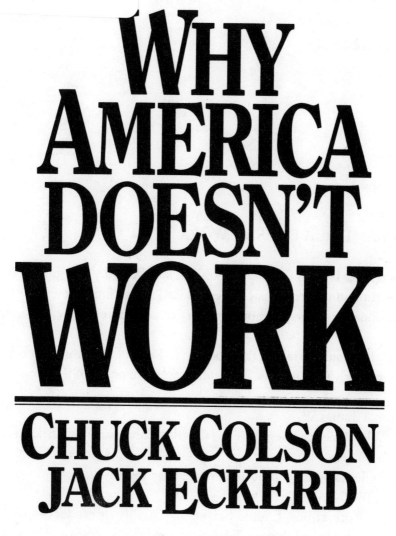

WHY AMERICA DOESN'T WORK

CHUCK COLSON
JACK ECKERD

WORD PUBLISHING

Dallas · London · Vancouver · Melbourne

WHY AMERICA DOESN'T WORK

All profits from the sale of this book go to Prison Fellowship and Eckerd Family Youth Alternatives. The authors receive no remuneration.

Colson, Charles W.
   Why America doesn't work / Charles Colson and Jack Eckerd.
     p. cm.
   Includes bibliographical references and index.
   ISBN 0–8499–0873–6
   1. Work ethic—United States. 2. Quality of products—United States. 3. United States—Economic conditions—1981–   I. Eckerd, Jack M., 1913– II. Title.
   HD8045.C65   1991
   306.3'613'0973—dc20   91-32864
                                                                      CIP

Printed in the United States of America

1 2 3 4 9 AGM 9 8 7 6 5 4 3 2 1

To our colleagues in Prison Fellowship and
Eckerd Family Youth Alternatives who exemplify
the work ethic and who labor selflessly on behalf
of others less fortunate.

Contents

Introduction

Someone may ask, "Why are Jack Eckerd and Chuck Colson writing a book on work?" Well, let us explain. As you will see shortly, we believe our country is in trouble. We have problems with productivity, standard of living, and the whole character of work, and we believe we know why.

Some of you may also be wondering, "What makes you two think you have answers? You're not economists."

That's certainly true. But, as you'll also soon see, the problem goes much deeper than the economy, into areas where we do have expertise.

Jack knows the marketplace. Starting with two drugstores, he built a business of seventeen hundred stores that employed thirty-five thousand men and women. He also knows government and bureaucracy; under President Gerald Ford he served as administrator of the General Services Administration, one of the largest government agencies. In his home state of Florida he has run PRIDE, one of the most successful prison industry programs in the world, while through his camps for disadvantaged children he has become more than familiar with our welfare and educational systems. He serves on the boards of numerous organizations, including Heritage Foundation, Hillsdale College, Culver Military, and Prison Fellowship

From his years as special counsel to former President Richard Nixon, Chuck knows government and bureaucracy and the way our country works—or more often doesn't work. And he knows prisons from the inside out and from working full time over the last fifteen years with Prison Fellowship.

Because of our friendship and mutual interests, we have worked together for more than ten years. During that time we have reached some strong convictions. The loss of the work ethic does not begin in the workplace; it begins in the hearts of people—in the values that motivate them or fail to motivate them. And here we both speak from our own firsthand experience of what the Christian life means to our values.

Throughout these pages you'll find us speaking with one voice, except where we need to identify our individual conclusions or experiences.

A True Parable

During World War II, those Jews who were not immediately exterminated by Hitler's brutal henchmen were herded into disease-infested concentration camps. In Hungary the Nazis set up a camp factory where prisoners were forced to distill tons of human waste and garbage into alcohol to be used as a fuel additive. Perhaps even worse than being forced to labor amid the nauseating odor of stewing sludge was the prisoners' realization that their work was helping to fuel the Führer's war machine. Yet month after month the laborers survived on meager food and disgusting work.

In 1944, Allied aircraft began bold air strikes deep into Europe. One night this area of Hungary was bombed, and the hated factory destroyed. The next morning the guards ordered the prisoners to one end of the charred remains where they were commanded to shovel the debris into carts and drag it to the other end of the compound.

They're going to make us rebuild this wretched place, the prisoners thought as they bent to their labor.

The next day they were ordered to move the huge pile of debris again, back to the other end of the compound.

Stupid swine, the prisoners murmured to themselves. *They made a mistake and now we have to undo everything we did yesterday.*

But it was no mistake.

Day after day the prisoners hauled the same mountain of rubble back and forth from one end of the camp to the other.

After several weeks of this meaningless drudgery, one old man began sobbing uncontrollably and was led away by the guards. Another screamed until his captors beat him into silence. Then a young man who had survived three years of the vile labor that supported the oppressors' cause darted away from the group and raced toward the electrified fence.

"Halt!" the guards shouted. But it was too late. There was a blinding flash, a terrible sizzling noise, and the smell of smoldering flesh.

The futile labor continued, and in the days that followed dozens of prisoners went mad and ran from their work, only to be shot by the guards or electrocuted by the fence.

Their captors didn't care, of course. Indeed the commandant of the camp had ordered this monstrous activity as "an experiment in mental health" to see what would happen when people were given meaningless work. After seeing the results, he smugly remarked that at this rate there soon would be "no more need to use the crematoria."

If you want to utterly crush a man, said the great Russian novelist Fyodor Dostoevsky in *The House of the Dead*, just give him work of a completely senseless, irrational nature.

Dostoevsky, who himself spent ten years in prison, wrote: "If he had to move a heap of earth from one place to another and back again—I believe the convict would hang himself . . . preferring rather to die than endure . . . such humiliation, shame and torture."

Deprived of meaningful work, men and women lose their reason for existence; they go stark, raving mad.[1]

PART 1

What Isn't Working?

The honest work of yesterday has lost its social status, its social esteem.

Peter Drucker[1]

1

Something's Not Working

It is necessary to develop the people's sense of labor, and this has to be done as soon as possible because for half a century no one [in the USSR] has found any reward in work. There is no one to grow wheat for bread, no one to take care of cattle. Millions are living in conditions that cannot be called dwelling, and they spent decades in stinking hovels. The elderly and invalids are poor as beggars. Roads are in terrible condition, and nature itself is taking revenge.

Aleksandr Solzhenitsyn[2]

PERCHED ON THE BRINK OF THE TWENTY-FIRST century, we look out across a land where our families are disintegrating, our streets have become drug-war combat zones, our classrooms are turning out thousands of functionally illiterate and morally bereft young people, our economy looks like it's on a roller-coaster, our government deliberately keeps millions idle, and our work force produces second-rate products while demanding first-rate benefits.

Things aren't working well here in America. The evidence is all around us. Too frequently, all you have to do is buy or use an American-made product.

Take the case of the missing wheel covers. Recently the Florida Highway Patrol added several top-of-the-line 1991 police cruisers to their fleets. These come equipped with powerful 350-cubic-inch V-8 engines, antilock brakes and "an annoying little problem." The plastic wheel covers keep falling off. So far the mystery hasn't been solved, since the covers seem to fly off—dangerous missiles hurtling through the air—at varying speeds. "We acknowledge that there is a problem with the wheel covers," said a company spokesman in a wonderful understatement. "The covers don't seem to have much endurance under adverse conditions."[3]

Now certainly any manufacturer can occasionally end up with a defective product or encounter a glitch that must be ironed out of a certain production model, but this kind of "annoying little problem" has become all too familiar in our country. Something has happened to America's pride and workmanship, and because of it we are often being whipped in world trade.

In most consumer ratings, American products consistently slip behind foreign competitors, and a recent study concluded that in 1990 the United States, alone among the seven great industrial nations of the world, suffered an actual decline in its real standard of living.[4]

Something is wrong.

Surveys reveal that fewer and fewer Americans want to work hard or take pride in what they do. Then there are the millions of citizens who don't—or won't—work. Five million people live in permanently subsidized unemployment, while our welfare rolls continue to swell.[5] Another million sit, bored and despairing, in overcrowded prisons, unable to contribute any economic support to either their families on the outside or to the bloated budgets required to support the prison system. And with all this, our crime rate is the highest in the free world.

The problem is so obvious that even a proudly liberal *New York Times* editorialist like Anna Quindlen acknowledges: "We are deeply dissatisfied with many of our social programs, if for no other reason than that they *do not work.* Education, welfare, crime have all come to seem like bottomless pits. Beneath them all is a black sea of poverty."[6]

Something is *very* wrong.

Americans have had every advantage. North America possesses an abundance of natural resources and fertile land for agriculture. In the prenuclear age, two oceans insulated us from the turmoil of Asia and Europe. Conquering the frontier bred a hardy stock of ruggedly independent men and women who fashioned a democracy that depended on the industry of every citizen. These forebears passed down to us a heritage of industry, thrift, diligence, and respect for property known as the work ethic. Based on that ethic, the world's noblest experiment in political and religious freedom created an economic machine that for over a century has been the marvel of the world.

But the very thing that made America great is in trouble today. Our economic engine is running down. We are losing the work ethic.

Ironically, we had to travel to the other side of the globe to have this brought forcefully home to us.

In March 1990, the two of us went to the Soviet Union as part of an American delegation sent to visit five Soviet prisons, including Perm 35, the Siberian outpost where many of the most notorious dissidents have been held. Our purpose was twofold: to share expertise about prisons with Soviet officials, and to press for the release of political prisoners.[7]

———

Every American enters the Soviet Union with conflicting emotions: excitement at passing through the once-impenetrable Iron Curtain and apprehension at what mysteries might lie beyond.

We were no exception as our blue-and-white Aeroflot jetliner, with its winged hammer-and-sickle insignia, began its descent into Moscow's Shermetovo Airport. Our tension, however, also carried an edge of fear. Within hours, if all went well, we would go where few Westerners had gone before: the Soviet gulag.

Grim-faced soldiers patrolled the airfield, watching us closely as we left the plane and entered the terminal. A serious young man in uniform checked our passports and visas, then waved us through to gather up our luggage and deal with the stone-faced customs officers. To our great surprise and relief the contents of our baggage didn't get a second glance.

The only thing that gave the airport officials pause was our destination: when the customs officer noted that our visit included the city of Perm, he stared at us, rolled his eyes, and repeated the word "Perm" several times with an odd, almost smug smile, as if to say, "Do you know what you're getting into?"

The first real hitch in the journey seemed to be the car in which we were to be transported to Moscow; the driver couldn't get it started. He cranked the engine of the black Volga over and over until, with a great belch of smoke, it finally sputtered to life. With the vehicle creaking and shaking as though it might break apart at the next jolt, we rattled off toward the city over roads pocked with potholes large enough to swallow a Lada, the plagiarized Fiat that serves as the "people's car." While the machinery of communism had been breaking down, apparently so had everything else.

As we approached the city, we began to understand why Irina Ratushinskaya, the Soviet poet and heroic dissident, had entitled her memoirs *Grey Is the Color of Hope.*

The Moscow skyline was gray. The soot-covered buildings with their heavy Cyrillic lettering were gray. The snow on the ground was gray. The leaden, omnipresent war monuments were gray. The heavily polluted air was gray. Even the people on the streets were gray—unsmiling, weighed down. Only the crimson epaulets on the soldiers' uniforms and the blazes of gold on the onion domes of the Kremlin stood out in vivid and welcome contrast.

Because we arrived a day ahead of the rest of the delegation, we had to fend for ourselves for the first twenty-four hours, getting at least a glimpse of ordinary Soviet life before we were ushered into the showcase of Soviet officialdom. We were booked into a typical tourist hotel, the Intourist in downtown Moscow, a tall modern-looking building—at least it was modern on the outside. Inside, it was chaos and confusion. People charged around the enormous, smoke-filled lobby in all directions, babbling in a dozen languages, while a half-naked dancer attempted to lure customers into the hotel bar and swarms of prostitutes openly worked the crowd.

At the reception desk we produced our prepaid vouchers, only to be told they had only one room reserved.

"We have vouchers here for two rooms," we said.

"The computer shows that you have only one room. Your travel agency made a mistake."

We had prepaid and had the evidence to prove it, but obviously in the Soviet system the customer was never right. We ended up paying over again for a second room and were sent up to what the desk clerk called our "deluxe rooms."

When we got to our floor—in an elevator that stopped short of the doorway by four or five inches—we could only wonder at the desk clerk's definition of deluxe. Even the dim lighting could not disguise the partially painted plywood panel walls; the faded and frayed carpets; the seedy, broken-down sofas; and the corroded bathroom fixtures that dripped incessantly. The beds were clean enough, but everything was in disrepair.

Finding a place to eat proved even more frustrating than getting a place to sleep.

Soviet law dictates that all visitors use only Soviet currency. People can be detained for giving out American dollars, and the Soviets keep a careful check on this by having visitors list all of their currency when they arrive and again when they leave. As members of an official delegation we dared not violate these rules. The problem was, the hotel restaurants refused to accept rubles; they all wanted our illegal American dollars.

Just as we were getting desperate enough to check out the Moscow McDonald's that we had passed on our drive in from the airport, we encountered an American, an assistant producer of the "Columbo" television show, who was there on holiday.

When we mentioned our dilemma, the friendly young man remarked, "I've been here five days and I've only had two decent meals. And those were at McDonald's. It's the only place you can get served and get enough to eat." Even in the restaurants food was scarce, he said, and you often had to bribe the maître d' to get a table, even in a half-empty dining room. After the black market, bribery was the biggest business in Moscow; everyone appeared to be on the take.

Our new acquaintance suggested we try the China Restaurant on the twentieth floor of the Intourist. "It's not great, but it's food," he said.

To this day we are uncertain what we ate that night—it was certainly not Chinese—but at least the place accepted rubles, and we could fill up on bread.

Before we retired, we tried to make a phone call to let our State Department contact know we had arrived. However, in Moscow you can't let your fingers do the walking because the Soviets do not have phone books. As a result, it's virtually impossible to locate anyone's phone number, and there are no operators to help. We ended that first night in the Soviet Union feeling that nothing worked, and what was worse, nobody cared.

The next day, Sunday, we made the transfer from tourists to official delegates, and the contrast could not have been more dramatic. A KGB official whisked us away in a polished black limousine, took us to a fine restaurant for a sumptuous meal with one lavish course after another (the communist bureaucrats can miss just about anything but their meals and vodka), and moved us to an "official" hotel where the opulent lobby had walls inlaid with rich mahogany paneling and marble floors covered with Persian rugs—though even here the escalators were broken. Our rooms were elegant, with commodious, tiled bathrooms and polished brass fixtures.

On Monday morning a caravan of black limousines hauled our delegation and its attendant luminaries to Domodedovo, the largest airport in the Soviet Union, serving all cities east of Moscow. We arrived at the airport about 9:30 and were told our flight would leave at 10:30.

At 10:40 they said, "Departure will be a bit late."

The plane finally took off at 1:30. Three hours later we landed in Perm.

The Ural Mountains form the boundary between the plains of European Russia and Asian Siberia, and just west of the spine of the Urals lies the industrial city of Perm. The capital of Oblensk, this city of 1.5 million people is a place of paralyzing drabness, several shades grayer than Moscow.

During the next day and a half we visited Perm 29, a traditional prison housing ordinary offenders, and Perm 35.

Certain names evoke powerful images and come to convey almost universal, generic meaning. Waterloo is synonymous with defeat, Benedict Arnold with betrayal, and gulag immediately conjures up oppression and "man's inhumanity to man." Perm Camp 35 is the crown jewel of the gulag.

Traveling over washed-out, sometimes flooded roads—evidence of the fact that it is still impossible to cross the USSR on a paved road—the bleak Siberian landscape fulfilled our every expectation. The late March winds chilled our bodies, and the sight of rough-strung barbed wire and guard towers bristling with guns made us uneasy.

Guards led us through huge gates and along a maze of pathways cut into the mountains of snow to a string of one- and two-story frame buildings that looked as though they dated back to the days of the czars.

Inside there was fresh paint everywhere, and everything appeared freshly scrubbed. Drab doors and walls had been hastily daubed with garish blue and green paint; in their zeal, they had even painted the floors.

Colonel Nikolai Osin, commandant at Perm 35 since 1972 and a man whose unfeeling eyes reflected equal contempt for visitors and inmates, herded us into a conference room where we were to interview several of the prisoners. Against three walls they had arranged chairs for the Soviet officials and our delegation; against the fourth wall sat a chair facing a television camera and glaring lights.

We protested this intimidating arrangement, but Osin was adamant. "It is the law," he insisted, wielding absolute authority over his sixty-one-acre kingdom.

With this arrangement, these men won't be able to tell us a thing, we thought.

But they did. While the KGB camera recorded their every word and expression, six of the most celebrated political prisoners in the world boldly told us the truth about the charges trumped up against them, how they had been denied their rights and had their visiting privileges canceled. At times they smiled almost defiantly at their captors as they sat in that lonely chair and exposed the horrors of the gulag. Some had spent as many as fifteen years in this brutal outpost. They spoke of lengthy solitary confinement for minor violations; one had been in solitary five times, while another had been kept there for twelve months. All complained that their mail had been tampered with and even blocked. At the end of the interview each thanked us and marched out of the room, shoulders squared, head high.

Aleksander Goldovitch, a physicist and an outspoken Christian, charged with treason for trying to row a rubber raft across the Black Sea to Turkey, asserted that they were prisoners of conscience. Later in his cold, cavelike, concrete cell he proudly pointed to a small cross he had etched in the cement above the door, a symbol of that faith which sustained him.

The Soviet system had done everything imaginable to beat these men into submission. Yet somehow in this hopeless outpost where one might expect to find a bleak, frozen winter of the spirit, these prisoners had kept their sense of individual dignity and purpose.

An amazing paradox.

We spent the remainder of our time back in Moscow, where we visited three more prisons, including the women's prison in Mozhaisk, a sprawling complex of brick and frame buildings holding nine hundred women convicted of offenses ranging from shoplifting to murder. Although conditions were austere, the officials boasted about such innovations as conjugal visits, furloughs, and release policies for pregnant women. They eagerly showed us their theater, education rooms, a well-stocked library with shiny, new leather-bound Bibles, and the mess hall.

We arrived at the mess hall just as lunch was being served. Some inmates were still passing through the line, having their trays filled; most were seated at long bench-style tables. Except for an occasional sideways glance, no one looked at us. Heads down, they kept eating.

Never one to be intimidated, Jack walked up to the line of women and asked casually, "How's the food?"

Oh, no! thought Chuck. *Now we're going to have to try this stuff.*

Sure enough, the commandant invited us to eat, and although the stew being slopped on the trays looked less than appetizing, we got in line. As we took our trays and sat at one of the tables and began to eat, the mood in the room changed dramatically. Women lifted their heads and looked at us; they began to point and chatter. One got up from her place and came over and sat next to us. She spoke excellent English, and as we chatted, others gathered around. One woman beamed widely, repeatedly pointing to a cross around her neck.

What amazed us in Mozhaisk, as in the other Soviet prisons we visited, was the fact that work seemed to be the heart of prison life. Every inmate had a job, six days a week, eight hours a day, and their production lines hummed with efficiency. At Perm we had seen most of the prisoners hard at work in various machine shops, where each had a production quota. With the money they earned they paid the cost of their confinement. At Mozhaisk we found a garment factory, where we spoke with a number of the women who were cutting and trimming fabric or running sewing machines. They appeared alert, interested in their work, some of them almost cheerful. Prison officials can disguise a lot of things with institutional whitewash, but not attitudes, and it was evident that morale was high in this place.

Each woman had a quota of four hundred pieces a day, for which she was paid 180 rubles a month, approximately two-thirds the average wage of a Soviet worker on the outside. The women told us that they were allowed to save money for their release or send it home. If they produced 10 percent more than their quota, they earned a bonus. Most worked overtime to do this. Could this be the initial signs of free enterprise?

No one knows the brutality of the Soviet prison system better than Aleksandr Solzhenitsyn, Nobel-Prize-winning writer and dissident who endured ten years in the gulag, often surviving on bare subsistence gruel while forced into hard labor in the frozen Siberian tundra. During his imprisonment he composed what would become *One Day in the Life of Ivan Denisovich*. In the classic novel, Solzhenitsyn recounts how backbreaking manual labor gave his life purpose. Even with his body stretched to the breaking point, he could feel a stab of pride when a gulag official looked over the rows of bricks he had laid and commended, "Good line."

Irina Ratushinskaya, the Soviet poet whose writings were pronounced subversive because they spoke of God and freedom, detailed her own gulag experience in her memoirs. In that bleak existence, full of deprivation and misery, her prison job making gloves provided a sense of purpose, occupied her mind, and gave meaning to her otherwise empty days.

Before we left the Soviet Union—a moment most visitors look forward to as much, or more, than their arrival—we walked the streets of Moscow and visited several stores. There we saw empty shelves and unsmiling people waiting in long lines for hours to buy the few products available. In a supermarket half the shelves were bare, and customers were lined up to buy small bags of vegetables and scrawny chickens. We saw no fruit of any kind and were told that everything was rationed, including sugar, salt, and even soap.[8]

Then our KGB escort drove us to the airport, bypassed the long lines at the ticket counters, and ushered us into a plush VIP lounge filled with top party and government officials.

"The hostess will escort you directly to your plane," he said, and with a half bow handed us our papers and passports.

While we waited for our flight, we sipped lemonade and nibbled from trays of caviar canapes, offered at ludicrously low prices. As we sat there talking, a well-dressed man stepped up and leaned against the counter next to us. He took a piece of paper from his pocket and began to read from it. As he did so, the waitress produced a bag of twelve lemons—as plump and juicy as any we'd ever seen in Florida's citrus groves—two huge eclairs dripping with thick chocolate, a large bag of cookies, and two one-pound bags of candy.

The man lined the goods up on the counter, checking off his shopping list, then handed the waitress a fifty ruble note—approximately eight dollars at the then official exchange rate but only two dollars on the black market.

Surely he can't buy all this for that amount, we thought.

Then we got an even greater shock. The waitress handed him thirty-five rubles in change!

This party member had just spent a trifling sum for a haul he could sell at an enormous profit on the booming Moscow black market, or he could stock the shelves of his *dacha,* the country estates made available to the ruling bureaucrats. While the ordinary citizens struggled for the barest essentials of life, government officials like this man—approximately five million of them—were living in the very best apartments, eating at their lavish restaurants, and shopping at their own well-stocked stores—where the prices have not been raised in decades!

On the plane we leaned back in our seats almost in stunned silence, reflecting on our recent experiences.

What we had seen was not only the collapse of socialism, but a society sick at heart. A society where the citizens walked the streets dejected and despairing. A society where hotel clerks and waiters didn't care whether they served you or had to be bribed to do so. A society riddled with crime and where suicide has become an increasing avenue of escape. A society where the black market is the only economy that works. We had seen a society suffering from the advanced stages of what the Danish philosopher Sören Kierkegaard called "soul sickness."

Then the irony hit us! For juxtaposed against all this were the images of the smiling, confident, determined men and women we had met behind the grim prison walls. The hope, industry, and productivity that had disappeared from the streets of Moscow seemed to be alive and well in the Soviet prisons.

It would have been natural for us to gloat over what we had seen. After all, we were both lifelong anticommunists, and Jack had been in the midst of an exciting free market economy that boomed in the fifties and sixties. Now, with the Soviet economy crumbling fast and the country's spirit sapped, the world was seeing the bankruptcy of socialism. The Soviet colossus was collapsing, and democracy, the free market, and capitalism had deservedly won the day.

But the disquieting parallels restrained us.

Weren't we seeing some of these same signs in America? Oh, to be sure, nothing like Moscow, but signs nonetheless—and troubling ones: workers producing and caring less; American-made products of poorer and poorer quality losing out in world markets; a growing privileged class; the spread between workers' and managements' salaries growing wider; rising crime and a deadly, entrenched welfare state.

As our plane touched down on American soil, we were grateful to be home, grateful to be Americans, but we also began to wonder whether we'd just seen a glimpse of our own future if we squander our heritage.

During the weeks following our visit to the Soviet Union, we had more than one conversation on this subject, and we became convinced we should write this book. Not just to look at what's wrong in America, but, more important, to offer some solutions.

We want to assure you that this is not just another hand-wringing diatribe. There are enough of those already.

We both have reputations as "can-do" people, and this is a "can-do" book: a book about what you can do to help restore the work ethic. Before we're done, we'll leave you with six principles that can change not only the way you work, but the way you live your life.

But be warned. We also have reputations for being straight talkers—blunt some would say. If at times we sound a little angry, that's because we are. And you should be too.

Because something is very wrong. America isn't working.

2

We're Number Five

As American productivity, once the exuberant engine of national wealth, has dipped to an embarrassingly uncompetitive low, Americans have shaken their heads: the country's old work ethic is dead.

Lance Morrow[1]

TWO YEARS AGO WHEN J. D. POWER AND Associates released its consumer satisfaction ratings for new cars, a model made by Buick ranked number five. It was the top American car on the 1989 list.

Since the Power Report is the industry's most respected and influential survey, General Motors immediately launched a major marketing campaign. Advertising dollars flowed. Posters were printed, and marketing kits were shipped to salespeople, touting the survey and enclosing reprints of articles from automobile magazines. Great news: *We're number five!*

Buick's hype demonstrated the sad plight of American automakers. Our companies are so used to landing at the bottom of the heap in reports of consumer satisfaction and quality that even number five sounded impressive.

In Power's 1989 rankings, for example, only four U.S. models were among the top twenty-one; and out of fifty-four models with below-average performance, fifty-three were American.[2]

Buick's gleeful campaign was short-lived. By 1991 the company had dropped to number nine. Japanese cars claimed five of the first seven spots on the list, while the Germans held the other two; the top U.S. automaker, Cadillac, posted a dismal number eight.[3]

Today the top-selling car in America is the Honda Accord, and the Japanese have now cornered 28 percent of the U.S. market. They have pulled this off largely by winning 46 percent of the buyers under the age of forty-five, an ominous statistic for the future. Japan's true rival for the American auto market is no longer Detroit, home of the first mass-produced automobile, but Europe with its finely crafted luxury models. American manufacturers are left to compete with imports from Korea and even Yugoslavia.

We literally can't keep up. It takes American car companies twice as long to bring a model from paper to the showroom floor. While the Japanese replace their old models an average of every four and a half years, with Honda turning around every four years, Detroit replaces its old models an average of every eight years.[4]

Unfortunately, the situation in the auto industry is just symptomatic of a much broader problem: in many basic industries we seem to be losing our share of the world market; we no longer manufacture products that are the envy of the world; and we are steadily losing ground to foreign competition. In 1965 the U.S. share of world exports was 27 percent; Japan's stood at about 7 percent. In 1986 the U.S. level had dropped to nearly 20 percent, almost the same level to which Japan's had risen.[5]

Some, like respected economist Herbert Stein, attribute this to currency fluctuations. When the dollar is strong, exports fall; when the dollar declines, as it did in 1986, exports increase.

Others argue that we are turning the situation around, pointing to the fact that U.S. companies are moving up slightly in the world's semiconductor market. Just a few years ago Japanese manufacturers refused to buy American silicon chips. Now they are doing so, having discovered that the quality and service of U.S. firms are improving.

It is true that we continue to dominate pharmaceuticals, light bulbs, x-ray equipment, and several other high-tech industries. And it can be taken as a positive that Boeing is still by far the world's largest manufacturer of aircraft.

But most economists believe that our competitive position has been steadily eroding and that we have held onto the market share we have largely because of technological superiority. Other countries have exported raw materials, while we've produced the sophisticated products.

One thing about which every expert agrees is that this technical know-how is critical to America's future in the world market. Yet even here there is evidence we are slipping.

Take the red-hot market for hand-held video cameras. Albert L. Sieg of Eastman Kodak says that because his company fell behind in its electronic imaging technology, they are losing market share to the Japanese. While Kodak is still promoting bulkier film technology, Japanese firms are building a more compact camera, breaking into America's yuppie market.[6]

These days the center for technical development shows signs of moving across the Pacific. American companies like Kodak, IBM, and Hewlett-Packard are setting up research laboratories overseas to get a step up on the technical breakthroughs.

This pattern is truly worrisome. In a 1991 survey of the competitive environment of twenty-four industrial nations and ten Third World countries, conducted by the International Management School of Lausanne, Switzerland, Japan—not the United States—ranked number one in an evaluation of 330 criteria, including economic strength, management, manufacturing excellence, resources, technology, and quality of work force.[7]

"Made in Japan" used to be a joke. Today it is no laughing matter.

Ross Perot, the gregarious billionaire entrepreneur, is one who isn't laughing: "In 1945 if someone had said that in our lifetimes Japan and Germany would be the industrial powers of the world, we would have thought he was crazy. But out of adversity comes strength, and they had no place to go but up. . . . As for America, we used to be king of the hill. We had the world's greatest economic engine. We could misspend money, waste money, and we had such an economic engine that we could always cover up our mistakes. . . . Well, we've lost our economic engine. In 1960 we made 75 percent of the world's cars—now we make 25 percent. The two largest exports from New York harbor today are scrap steel and scrap paper going to Japan."[8]

Another of those not laughing is William Brock who, after his tenure as secretary of labor under Ronald Reagan, was part of a blue-ribbon committee for a study on productivity. Drawing on representatives from business, government, labor, and education, this commission published a report called *America's Choice: High Skills or Low Wages,* which came to the chilling conclusion that "America is headed toward an economic cliff."[9]

From 1960 to 1973, according to this report, American private, nonagricultural workers each produced an average of 2.9 percent more every year than the year before. Since 1973 that average has dropped to less than 1 percent. It now takes nearly three years to achieve the same productivity improvement we used to achieve in one year, and that rate is half of what it was twenty years ago.

If productivity continues to falter, the "America's Choice" commission speculates, we can expect one of two consequences. Either the top third of our population will grow wealthier while the bottom two-thirds becomes progressively poorer, or "we will slide into relative poverty together."[10]

Indications of that slide are already evident. Since 1969 average weekly earnings in constant dollars have fallen by more than 12 percent. Family income is up, but not because of an increase in individual wages. Instead it is the result of an increase in two-earner households, an arrangement that many families now find essential, but which could have a negative impact on the workplace and the family. Two-earner households are, in part, the cause of smaller families, and studies show that because of this trend in the baby boom generation, entries to the work force will begin slowing in the 1990s.

There is little reason to hope that the current slide in the marketplace can be reversed. For as government and private studies alike conclude, our educational system is failing miserably to prepare young people for today's competitive world. The situation is so alarming that a 1991 report from the Department of Labor's Commission on Achieving Skills concluded that "More than half of our young people today leave school without the knowledge or foundation required to find and hold a job. . . . Many of these youth will never be able to earn a decent living."[11]

Economists disagree about the underlying economic factors that account for these disturbing trends. Tax structures, new antitrust regulations, even environmental regulations affect productivity, and statistical comparisons between nations are skewed by fluctuating exchange rates and even cost-of-living factors. Suffice it to say that there are almost as many explanations for America's current plight as there are experts.

As we said earlier, we are not economists. We won't pretend to give an economic analysis of America's apparent woes. But we do know this. We will never fully understand American industry until we take our eyes off the boardrooms and look at the front lines: the production lines, the assembly lines, the unemployment lines. In other words, we need to look at the working people—the economy's most important asset.

In the years immediately following World War II, American industry made what it now admits was a major misjudgment.

Proving the adage that a prophet is without honor in his hometown, American business turned a deaf ear to the innovative labor management concepts of an American engineer named W. Edwards Deming. So Deming took his ideas about team management, training, and the development of workers to Japan. Even Deming's harshest critics now concede that these ideas contributed greatly to the astonishing revitalization and success of Japanese industry.

While Japan accepted and employed Deming's team management approach—a method that depended on bringing workers into the decision-making process—American manufacturers, for the most part, retained an autocratic form of management.

The Japanese are blunt in their assessment of American industry. "American executives are too aristocratic," observes one Japanese industrialist. "Very few of them have ever worked on a production line themselves, and they have little or no contact with their workers whom they treat as interchangeable parts."[12]

Granted, the Japanese have their own employee-management difficulties. Long Japanese workdays are reported to have a negative effect on the family, and anecdotal evidence connects excessive work stress with illness and even suicide.

American managers too often greet new technologies not as ways to improve production but as a means of monitoring and intimidating employees who perform repetitious tasks—what one writer calls the "electronic whip." From 10 to 26 million employees now have their work tracked by some form of electronic surveillance, such as counting keystrokes. This can be dehumanizing when not accompanied by improved employer-employee interaction.

"In Japan, we value all of our workers," says a Japanese plant manager. "We pay our assembly worker on the same basis as our engineer—how workers individually contribute to the final product—and we provide him with the same amount of training. America is now more a country of economic hierarchy than Japan."[13]

Evidence of this abounds. Even during the 1990–91 economic recession, many corporate CEOs received fat raises as dividends and profits fell. At a time when workers were being asked to sacrifice jobs and benefits, CEOs were piling up huge compensation packages. At a recent Senate hearing, an expert in industrial relations and compensation testified: "The pay of CEOs and senior executives of American companies seems to be spiraling out of control." While "the chief executive of a Japanese company earns about 17 times the pay of an average worker . . . in the United States, some CEOs are paid 109 times more than the average worker when salaries, bonuses and stock options are included."[14]

Take the case of General Dynamics: the company lost $500 million and laid off twenty-seven thousand workers—and for this CEO William Anders was rewarded with $800,000 in salary and $4 million in stock options. Or consider Stephen Wolfe, who as CEO of United Airlines was paid more than $18.3 million in salary, bonuses, and stock incentives in 1990, a year when his airline's profits plunged by 71 percent and flight attendants had gone four straight years without a raise. No less a defender of the free market than *Forbes* says plainly, "It doesn't make sense."[15]

Sometimes management seems blind to the message it sends to its workers. In 1989 when the U.S. Postal Service was under intense pressure to hold rates in line and improve productivity, those running the service, who enjoy cushy salaries and almost guaranteed job security, spent more than $6.2 million on conferences.

Not surprisingly, postal officers decided to hold these during winter months at tropical sites. At one such gathering, conference goers downed $99 dinners at taxpayers' expense; their beverage tab alone came to a whopping $12,718. According to the General Accounting Office, the daily costs for food and drink per executive at another conference averaged between $109 and $137. All that planning to raise the public's postal rates evidently works up quite a thirst.[16]

In the fiscal year 1990 the Postal Service incurred a huge deficit; notwithstanding, executives at Postal Service headquarters, directors of five regional offices, and seventy-three division postmasters received bonuses averaging more than $5,900 per year.[17]

Now granted, the Postal Service is a government-protected monopoly and therefore somewhat apart from mainstream business. However, management insensitivity—the kind of thing Edward Deming preaches against—contributes to a major attitude problem in the American workplace, of which postal workers are certainly a part. This kind of behavior sends a message to the rest of the employees, who, justifiably resentful, begin to think, *Why should I work hard when these fat cats are out playing?*

Resentment can quickly infect a work force, creating general cynicism and apathy—which is yet another cause of poor productivity.

A recent survey found that 43 percent of all workers could be classed as cynical. They don't trust management or their coworkers; they don't think their pay is fair or that they have a fair shot at advancement; they don't believe management listens to them or values what they do on their jobs. They assume management is only "out for themselves" and therefore see no reason to improve their own performance on the job. Like all of us, these workers are motivated by personal gain of one form or another, and nothing indicates to them that increased performance will net them anything in return.[18]

A Lou Harris poll of one furniture manufacturer's employees reveals how dangerous this cynicism can be: 87 percent said that "honest, ethical, upright management" was very important; but only 38 percent said it was true of their own employers. Employees with this cynical view of their own companies are not likely to be efficient or productive.[19]

Alienating workers from management also creates inefficiency. "We have as much bureaucracy in some of our businesses as we have in Washington," says William Brock, and there is a reason. "By de-emphasizing the quality of workers, we have to increase the number of supervisors. What a waste."[20]

Bureaucracy and cynicism harden attitudes on both sides. Even today after Deming's theories have been tried and proven in Japan, America's cynical workers are reluctant to adopt them. George Kourpias, president of the 740,000-member International Association of Machinists (IAM), recently issued a paper to every local union in the IAM telling them to "vigorously resist" any team concept program because such programs undermine the union's duty to protect the interests of its members.[21]

As the IAM attitude indicates, not all the responsibility lies with management. There is plenty of blame to be shared on both sides of the bargaining table. Management may have been cavalier, but labor has hardly been a model of restraint. It was Kourpias's intransigent union that pushed Eastern Airlines over the edge, costing its own members thousands of jobs. There have been repeated instances when unions became so intractable they nearly broke the companies that provided jobs for their own members.

Whether caused by autocratic management practices, labor unions, or worker cynicism, one fact is indisputable: Our rate of productivity is in trouble because we are working less. A University of Michigan study, for example, discovered that between 1965 and 1975 the amount of time workers actually spent on the job decreased by 10 percent.[22]

The U.S. Postal Service offers a striking example of this trend. It recently invested $5 billion in automatic sorting equipment, which should have increased productivity. But those gains were offset by the time spent on "nonproductive activities"—like taking breaks, clocking in and out, and shuffling empty trays and carts. In 1969 nonproductive time accounted for 5.8 percent of a postal worker's day; this translated into $118 million in wages. In 1989 workers spent 19 percent of their day on nonproductive activities, costing taxpayers $1.82 billion per year. Yet earlier this year Postal Service officials, refreshed from their tropical conferences, lobbied furiously for a 19 percent increase in rates.[23]

This leads us to what may be the most critical question: Does this reduced work effort reflect less motivation on the part of the individual worker? What are the values and attitudes of the man and woman standing at the lathe or making data entries or loading a van? After all, what individuals think about their jobs, their standards of performance, and their pride in their work are the factors that make the difference in both quality and output.

Lou Harris found that 63 percent of our workers believe that people don't work as hard as they did ten years ago; 78 percent say that people are taking less pride in their work; 69 percent think workmanship is inferior; and 73 percent believe workers are less motivated.[24]

Americans aren't working much, and they aren't working well.

When he was chairman of the Federal Reserve Board, the late Arthur Burns acknowledged the difficulty of explaining declining productivity, but his own conclusion went right to the heart of the matter: "My own judgment is that we've been undergoing a change in our societal values and attitudes that has contributed significantly to poorer job performance in recent years."[25]

Declining rates of productivity . . . the loss of competitive position in some world markets . . . workers who aren't working. It's a bleak picture.

What has happened to the industry and productivity that made this country the marvel of the industrialized world?

Since the beginning of our nation, Americans have understood these truths to be self-evident—that thrift, industry, diligence, and perseverance are all qualities to be cultivated and respected in society. It's called the work ethic, and these are the American ideals that set us apart for centuries.

America's drive to work well and to work hard was more than simply good business; it was rooted in the same deep religious commitment that first brought settlers to the New World.

From the sturdy Scottish Protestants to the Italian Catholics and enterprising Jewish immigrants, from the tiny country churches to the synagogues and grand cathedrals of the city parishes, America was built by a religious people. And one of the basic beliefs that they brought with them was that, in the words of one modern writer, "their work mattered to God."[26]

So what has happened? Arthur Burns got to the heart of the problem: our societal values and attitudes have changed dramatically.

We promised that this would not be another book of hand wringing and despair. It isn't. Because we can recover the work ethic—and we'll tell you how. But first we have to understand what it is, where it came from, and how we lost it.

PART 2

Whatever Became of the Work Ethic?

Has the American work ethic really expired? Is some old native eagerness to level wilderness and dig and build and invent now collapsing toward a decadence of dope, narcissism, income transfers and aerobic self-actualization?

Lance Morrow[1]

3

The Roots of Work

Man is made to be in the visible universe an image and likeness of God Himself, and he is placed in it in order to subdue the earth. From the beginning therefore he is called to work.

Pope John Paul II[2]

All men were created to busy themselves with labor . . . for the common good.

John Calvin[3]

For BETTER OR FOR WORSE, OUR WORK defines us. To paraphrase Descartes, there is a sense in which we work, therefore we are. "So what do you do?" is usually the first question we ask upon meeting a new acquaintance.

Work is one of the few constants of our existence, one of the few commonalities of humanity, and we spend about half of our waking life doing it. Work is also the best indicator of the vitality

31

of an individual or civilization. Why else would unemployment and productivity figures be some of the first statistics on everyone's lips when assessing the health of our national economy?

However, work is much more than the sum of these parts. It is much more than just a need to keep busy or bring home a paycheck. Meaningful work is a fundamental dimension of human existence, an expression of our very nature. Without it, we can go stark, raving mad, as the Nazi concentration camp experiment demonstrates in our opening parable. It is this innate need and drive for meaning and significance that kept the men and women in the Soviet prisons and labor camps sane, proud, and purposeful. Set within us from the beginning, this purposeful nature drives us to work hard, to be productive, to create, and to accumulate the results of our labor.

Work is thus a moral imperative, which is the source of *ethic* in *work ethic*—probably one of the most misunderstood terms in the English language.

While what we term the *work ethic*—commonly called the *Protestant work ethic*—is largely credited by many with industrializing the West and fueling America's incredible economic growth, for many people it conjures up simple notions about hard work or images of black-robed Puritans who preached about God as the great taskmaster cracking his whip over poor humanity.

But the work ethic that originally made America strong is not simple axioms, nor is it the sole province of Protestantism. And it traces its roots much further back in history than the Puritans.

———

From the beginning of the world there was work, for at the beginning there was Creation—the work of God. When he rested on the seventh day, "he rested from *all the work* of creating he had done" and God pronounced his work "good."[4]

God created human beings in his own image, and part of

being "in his image" means that we are workers, like God himself. That's where that innate, inner drive comes from.

God called mankind to cultivate the world he had created and to exercise dominion over it. This was a call to work, to perform both manual labor (pruning the trees and tilling the fields) and intellectual labor (naming the animals); one was not set above the other as greater or more important—a mistake frequently made by subsequent civilizations.

This high view of labor, with its just compensation resulting in private property, was encoded and enshrined in the Ten Commandments: "Six days you shall labor and do all your work. . . . You shall not steal. . . . You shall not covet your neighbor's house . . . his ox or donkey, or anything that belongs to your neighbor."[5]

To the ancient Jews "work was life," and they had a saying: "He who does not teach his son a trade teaches him to steal." Although their training made them the equivalent of college professors, the Jewish rabbis did not accept money for teaching. Each learned a trade at which he worked with his hands and by which he supported himself. Rabbis were tailors and shoemakers and barbers and bakers and even performers.[6]

For the Jew, work was a gift from God. "It is good and proper for a man . . . to find satisfaction in his toilsome labor under the sun . . . to accept his lot and be happy in his work—this is a gift of God."[7]

This was a radical notion, contrary to the prevailing wisdom of the great pagan civilizations of the day. Most Greeks considered work a curse. The gods hated mankind, Homer argued, and out of spite condemned man to toil.[8] The Greeks called work "ponos," from the Latin *poena*, meaning "punishment." Artisans and craftsmen were regarded as little better than slaves, while slavery itself was an institution based on a loathing of work.

Plato and Aristotle promoted a two-story concept of work—that the majority of men should do the heavy lifting so that the minority, like themselves, might engage in higher pursuits such as art, philosophy, and politics. Across the Adriatic, Cicero allowed that for Romans there were only two worthy occupations: agriculture and big business, especially if these could lead to a comfortable retirement.

Christianity changed all of this.

In many ways Christianity has always been a working man's faith. As a carpenter in Nazareth, Jesus worked with his hands, and the followers he drew were working people who rose before dawn to drag smelly fishing nets through the waters of Galilee to earn a living.

The early Christians were working-class folks who, raised in the Judaic tradition, abhorred idleness and made work a requirement of the early church. "If a man will not work," the Apostle Paul said bluntly, "he shall not eat."[9] And those who did work were to share the results of their labor with the needy. Many New Testament passages urge the followers of Christ to use their gifts for the service of others—and the early Christians did so.

Nor did the early Christians share the Greek's two-story distinction between mental and physical work. After all, the Son of God himself, in his brief years as a human being, had been a carpenter, while the Apostle Paul, a rabbinical scholar, paid his own way by making tents.

As one historian notes: "Christianity undercut slavery by giving dignity to work, no matter how seemingly menial that might be. Traditionally, labor which might be performed by slaves was despised as degrading to the freeman. Christian teachers said that all should work and that labor should be done as to Christ as master and as to God and in the sight of God. Work became a Christian duty. Before the end of the fifth century slavery was declining."[10]

When the barbarian hordes overran Western civilization, this high view of work was preserved in the monastic communities to which Christianity retreated. Carrying out the commandment to work, the industrious monks built enclaves of industry, learning, scholarship, and beauty. They drained the swamps, built bridges and roads, and invented labor-saving devices. They copied the sacred writings, produced works of art in illuminated manuscripts, and kept faith and scholarship alive. In each of these pursuits they heeded Augustine's exhortation that *laborare est orare,* "to work is to pray."

During the late Middle Ages a form of voluntary association, called the guild, grew up among the workers. Designed to promote the common interest of workers, these guilds also set standards for good workmanship, encouraged active participation in civic affairs, expected moral behavior, and often required faithful religious observance. The guilds maintained high ethical standards for approving weights and measures, and the members prided themselves that nothing would leave their shops that was not of the highest quality. Workers began taking satisfaction not only in the results of their own labor, but in their fellow guildsmen's work as well.

This high view of work was also prevalent among the great artists of the Renaissance and Baroque periods. Johann Sebastian Bach inscribed the letters SDG on the bottom of his compositions, standing for *Sola Deo Gloria* ("to the glory of God alone"). With the same motivation, Albrecht Dürer carved his woodcuts and engravings, and Michelangelo and Rembrandt sculpted and painted.

The true foundation of Europe's magnificent cathedrals was not stone, but the understanding that work was a collaboration with God. That was why the builders stationed angels at the heights; they knew God saw what they were doing and cared.

Unfortunately this was not the only view of work preserved through these centuries, for a vestige of Greek dualism persisted. Monastic orders divided themselves into lay brothers, who did the manual labor, and those who pursued the higher or intellectual tasks.

Then one man, with great determination and courage, shook the ethos of the Middle Ages—religious, political, social, and economic—to its very foundations with his seemingly radical ideas.

When Martin Luther strode into downtown Wittenberg on a late autumn day in 1517, he was a relatively unknown Augustinian cleric. Puzzled burghers and merchants watched as this lecturer in philosophy from the local university walked briskly up to the Castle Church and nailed a piece of parchment to the door containing ninety-five theses "for the purpose of eliciting truth." Luther's notice nailed October 31, 1517, on the calendar forever.

Most make the mistake of seeing the Reformation strictly in theological terms. It's true that Luther's confrontation changed the church, and despite the schism created, the people of God in both Catholic and Protestant traditions have been strengthened as a result. But equally profound and more relevant for our purposes here have been the consequences in the political, social, and economic realms.

Politically, the Reformation set the church free of the iron grip of the state. Challenging the divine rule of kings, it planted the seeds of democracy and the rule of law.

Socially, the Reformation struck at society's dualistic view of work. Just as they saw the church comprised of all the people of God, not just the clergy, so the Reformers saw all work—sacred and secular, intellectual and manual—as a way of serving God.

The work of monks and priests, wrote Luther, "in God's sight are in no way whatever superior to the works of a farmer laboring in the field, or of a woman looking after her home."[11] The view that scrubbing floors held as much dignity as occupying the pulpit democratized the work ethic.

Thus the Reformers—German, Dutch, English, and Swiss—encouraged people to abandon the isolation of the cloisters and enter the world of work. What mattered was that each individual understood his or her calling or vocation; in that way they collaborated with God in the grand design of the universe, working for his glory, the common good, and their own fulfillment.

The notion that people should abandon inherited trades and do whatever would maximize their worth to God served to further break down the rigid caste divisions in both the church and society.

This teaching about vocation also challenged existing social values by encouraging care for others. As Luther wrote: "Man does not live for himself alone . . . but he lives also for all men on earth." In this vein Calvin encouraged workers to produce more than they needed so they could give surpluses to those in need.

All this drastically affected the economic situation of the day, paving the way for what we have come to know as democratic capitalism. Until the Reformation, the church viewed most forms of trade carried on for profit as inherently immoral. But the Reformers maintained that all work, including that of the tradesman or businessman, could be pleasing to God. Business was liberated, providing the essential incentives for the work ethic and thus fueling the great industrial revolution of the West.[12]

The feudal establishment was not amused by these radical doctrines, which spread like wildfire across Europe. In fact, one of the charges of heresy against English Reformer William Tyndale was that he taught: "If we look externally, there is a difference betwixt the washing of dishes and preaching the Word of God; but as touching to please God, in relation to His call, none at all."[13]

Such teachings freed people to do what they did best for God's glory, and a new breed of workers was born. Out of religious conviction these men and women sought excellence and shunned idleness, vanity, and waste as deadly sins.

To ignore the religious roots of the work ethic is to ignore the clear evidence of history. But we should also note that it is not sectarian.[14] It represents a truth that has universal application in any society willing to accept it.[15] But without doubt its most impressive track record has been in Europe and America.

———

The most precious cargo carried by the shiploads of immigrants who set sail for the New World seeking religious freedom and economic opportunity was their view of work. Primarily Puritans and Quakers, they came "as laborers for their Lord, straighteners of crooked places, engaged in a task filled with hardship, deprivation and toil."[16]

Contrary to what is often supposed, the much-maligned Puritans did not seek wealth as the ultimate reward, neither did they make the mistake of some moderns and worship work itself. They worshiped God—what cultural critic Os Guinness calls the "audience of one"—through their work, which enabled them to treat success with equanimity and failure without regret.

Nor did the Puritans regard wealth as a badge of piety (as many television preachers do today). Wealth and possessions could be a blessing, a testing, or even an abandonment to one's own covetousness. Prosperity could also be evidence of Satanic attack. The Puritans viewed work as stewardship to God, which made their primary rewards spiritual and moral.[17]

"Choose that employment or calling in which you may be most serviceable to God," said Puritan writer Richard Baxter. "Choose not that in which you may be most rich or honorable in the world; but that in which you may do most good, and best escape sinning."[18]

The Puritans came to the New World to demonstrate, as William Penn wrote, "what sobriety and industry can do in a wilderness against heat, cold, wants and dangers." Thus hard work and determination became equated with the moral life, and out of this they fashioned a new land with a new ethic.

As a result, the virtue of work became as deeply ingrained in American culture as democracy. Over succeeding generations this ethic produced a thriving society and later fueled the industrial revolution which produced vast increases in invention, productivity, and wealth.

Unfortunately, spiritual movements follow almost predictable cycles: They unleash a force that society first embraces and then in due course profanes.

In Europe during the late eighteenth and early nineteenth centuries, this cycle stripped the work ethic of its distinctively Christian character. Workers were exploited, giving rise to work-houses, debtors' prisons, and child labor.

Yet these excesses aroused still another spiritual movement that rose to counter man's inhumanity to man. Men like William Wilberforce and Lord Shaftsbury successfully launched a wave of reforms in the workplace and labored tirelessly for years to bring about the abolition of slavery.

In America the distinctively Christian work ethic was preserved until the mid-nineteenth century. As immigrants poured across our shores, it was hard work that allowed them to leave the slums and factories behind for a more prosperous life. "For millions of Americans, as they labored through the complexities of generations, work worked," says Lance Morrow, until the immigrant work ethic "came at last to merge with the Protestant work ethic."[19]

But then the ethic began to erode, partly because of the very society it helped to create. In the view of one writer, this loss was directly connected with the rise of a technical civilization: "The calling lost its vertical bearings in the incessant whirr of machinery and the grime of the mill town. . . . As the modern world awoke to its material strength and shook off the disciplines of the Puritan way of life, it found that the doctrine of the secular calling had become unnecessary. . . . Vocation became simply 'occupation.'"[20]

The result was a hollowed-out version of the work ethic. People still worked hard but for different reasons. God was no longer the sacred object of man's labors; instead, labor itself became the shrine. A typical exponent of this new *secular ethic* was Calvin Coolidge, who said, "He who builds a factory builds a temple, and he who works there, worships there."[21]

So deeply ingrained was the work ethic in the American psyche, however, that this "good old all-American" version continued to preserve the essential virtues of honest work, thrift, investment, savings, respect of property, and charity toward others. Even if they didn't believe it their godly duty, people still taught their children these values because they realized that at heart they were what cherished and sanctified the great American dream.

Thus the work ethic survived. Until the revolution . . .

4

The Revolution

Nobody gets out of here alive.

Jim Morrison, The Doors

T HE 1960s MAY WELL HAVE PRODUCED THE greatest cultural and social revolution in American history. Less bloody perhaps, but in some ways as significant as the Civil War, this decade transformed America's view of the world, of the nature of life, of reality itself.

For twenty-three centuries Western civilization held fast to certain transcendent truths by which the affairs of individuals and nations were determined. This prevailing wisdom dated back to the Greeks and Romans. To Plato, who argued that society couldn't survive without an ultimate source of authority; to Cicero, who maintained that justice and concord among people would be impossible without God.

When Christianity took root in Western culture, it adapted and transformed these beliefs, and this alliance of Jerusalem and Athens remained the dominant intellectual and social influence until the eighteenth and nineteenth centuries.

In the eighteenth century, with the rise of what was called the Enlightenment, viewed as the dawn of human reason, the forces of nature, the organization of society, and the character of morality were all radically reinterpreted. Then in the nineteenth century Darwin dispensed with the need for God to understand man's origins and the order of creation; Freud explained religion as a purely human construction; and Nietzsche and Marx argued that man was now free to be master of his own universe. Some attempted to reconstruct a moral consensus by appealing to "self-evident truths" or "enlightened self-interest," and all sought to build new structures of morality without reference to divine will or traditional law.

Thus, for the first time in Western history the intellectual world contended it was possible to create a just order without God.

Although philosophers and intellectuals debated them, these ideas did not really penetrate the popular consciousness. Most people still went to church and lived their lives according to the deeply entrenched traditions and values of Judeo-Christian culture.

Until this century, that is, when these ideas began to influence a wide cross section of people. Eminent historian Paul Johnson pinpoints 1919 and Einstein's discovery of relativity as the decisive time and event; thereafter, he argues, relativity in the physical sciences became confused with relativism in the field of ideas. Perhaps.

But it was in the sixties that the vanguard of the revolution invaded American college campuses and swept through every area of popular culture.

Most Americans probably do not fully comprehend what happened in that tumultuous decade. We tend to think of the flower children and the hippies as a passing phenomenon, a reaction against the apathy of the fifties, a protest against an unpopular war, a typical, though excessive, youthful rebellion against all authority. Kids will do their thing, we say; they've grown up now and life is back to normal. Well, that's only partially true.

Because the long-haired flower children and drug-dazed hippies were only draftees in the revolution. They served their time at

Berkeley and Woodstock, and then most went home. The generals of the revolution, however, are still with us, and millions, albeit unconsciously, now march to their drums.

{The generals were the cultural elite who saw the youthful fervor and rebellion of the sixties as an opportunity to usher in their own new age of enlightenment. For them it was a world in which, as the cover of *Time* magazine proclaimed, "God is dead," and man was finally his own master, cut loose from twenty-three centuries of an oppressive, tradition-bound, Western ethos.}

French writer and philosopher Albert Camus, whose works focus on a world without God, a world in which life is meaningless, death arbitrary, and man stands alone under sentence of death, trying to make the best of it, became one of the most popular writers of the day.

Camus proclaimed his philosophy, which would also become the message of the sixties, when he spoke to Columbia University students in 1946: "Born and bred in such a world, what did we believe in? Nothing. Nothing except the obstinate negation in which we were forced to close ourselves from the very beginning. The world in which we were called to exist was an absurd world, and there was no other in which we could take refuge."[1]

Camus's close associate, Jean-Paul Sartre, articulated a similar philosophy: "Every existing thing is born without reason, prolongs itself out of weakness, and dies by chance."

While these men utterly rejected God, they recognized that humanity could not survive in the vacuum of such a world. In the absence of God, we all worship some god—money, power, lust, or something else; we all make individual choices that reflect what we value most. For Camus and his colleagues, that alternative source of meaning became man himself. "I still believe the world has no transcendent meaning," Camus said. "But I know that something in it has a meaning and that is man."

Since the universe was ultimately evil, any goodness had to be found in man; so Camus called men and women to revolt against this threatening world and to "humanize the inhuman"—to transform the inhumanity of the world into the image of man. Man as his own God became the creed of the revolutionaries—not really a new idea since it dates back to the Garden of Eden.

In the sixties this became a rallying cry for those already influenced by the beat generation, with its heroes like road-warrior Jack Kerouac, and the "antiestablishment" movement was born. In their individualized pursuit of pleasure and "peace," the adherents turned on, tuned in, and dropped out. "If it feels good, do it," became the order of the day, and drugs were the avenue of choice, a quick and easy path to a bogus enlightenment fostered by LSD-laced gurus like Timothy Leary. "No hope without dope" and "Better living through chemistry" became popular slogans.

If dope was hope, sex was salvation. Responding to the ritual chants of "free love" and "make love not war," eager acolytes cast traditional restraints aside. Marriage became "just a piece of paper," a belch from an uptight past when people thought sex was dirty and adultery sinful. Every sort of alternate arrangement was acceptable, as long as it was not the traditional one.

Dostoevsky wrote, "If there is no God, everything is permitted," and the sixties are a testament to the truth of that statement. The sixties became hedonism on steroids.

But the antiestablishment movement didn't stop with drugs and sex. The right to "do your own thing" meant all barriers had to fall, and with the restraints loosened, political radicalism burst forth on campuses all across America. These revolutionaries weren't just trying to reform curricula or protest Vietnam; they were organizing a wholesale assault on all "bourgeois, middle-class values." To do this, they had to seize power from the corporations and create a "society that will be able to function without the incentives of the market economy," as one writer put it.[2]

The quintessential symbol of the 1950s had been the man in the gray flannel suit who scaled the corporate ladder during the day and retreated to the sanctity of his suburban three-bedroom rambler at night. To the radicals of the sixties this represented capitalism, which was responsible for "the continuing semi-colonial status of negroes, the emptiness and boredom of 'affluence,' the neo-colonial war in Vietnam, the commercialization of all aspects of life, the stream of lies about the purpose and function of American institutions."[3]

These views, although advanced by radicals, seeped into the culture and began to influence, almost unconsciously, popular values on a wide scale.

In this attack on tradition, nothing came under more intense assault than the work ethic. One writer of the 1960s spoke glowingly of the vision "of a practical culture in which man is free from labor, free to begin at last the historic task of constructing truly human relationships."[4]

By the early seventies, Studs Terkel, self-proclaimed spokesman for American values, pronounced the demise of the work ethic in the opening words of his book, *Working:* "This book being about work is, by its very nature, about violence—to the spirit as well as to the body." In gathering his material, Terkel interviewed 133 people whom he discovered to be singing either "The Blue Collar Blues" or "Groaning the White Collar Moans."

"It is only the happy few," he said, "who find a savor in their job."[5]

In a mere decade, the popular culture and student radicalism spawned by the existentialist writers had succeeded in bringing Western civilization full circle. Once again work had become a dirty word—something one did only if one must pay for pleasure. Work was no longer ennobling; it was again utilitarian—simply a means to an end.

Ironically, one of the first to see what the great cultural revolution had done to the work ethic and other basic Western values was not one of our countrymen, but a tortured citizen from the land of Perm 35.

———

Harvard's ivy-covered yards were alive with august crimson-robed faculty and euphoric students on that warm spring day as they gathered for the 1978 commencement address, given as usual by one of the world's greats. This year it was one of the twentieth century's most revered writers, a bearded, shaggy-haired Russian whose face bore a toughness etched by experiences no one in the audience could comprehend.

Imprisoned in the dark outposts of the gulag, Aleksandr Solzhenitsyn had practically worshiped the West. Now, he declared to the company before him, he was profoundly disturbed by what this country had become. How, he wondered, had this great land "declined from its triumphal march to its present decline?"

The West had done well, he said, at providing freedom and material goods, but its people now linked the acquisition of these goods to what they called "happiness" in the debased sense of the word. There was freedom, to be sure, but it was being perverted into license, "a freedom toward evil."

And what did Solzhenitsyn believe was at the root of this?

In the early democracies, including America, human rights were granted on the ground that man is God's creature. Freedom, Solzhenitsyn said, was given conditionally, with the assumption of constant religious responsibility. But now he perceived "a total emancipation from the moral heritage of the Christian centuries with their great reserves of mercy and sacrifice."

The West had finally achieved the rights of man, the great Russian writer warned, "but man's sense of responsibility to God and Society has grown dimmer and dimmer." Precisely what had happened in the sixties revolution.

The literate, intelligent Harvard throng should have welcomed this astute cultural critique from a literary figure of such stature, especially given the price he had paid for his wisdom. But Solzhenitsyn's diagnosis did not sit at all well in the hallowed precincts of Cambridge. As his fellow citizens had learned in the USSR, talking about God can be dangerous!

The bell-bottoms and lank hair of the sixties gave way years ago to the dress-for-success garb of corporate America. Today, in the face of AIDS—and maybe from sheer exhaustion—even free love has become costly enough to yield to "the new monogamy." So, we ask again, were the sixties just a fad?

Well, the styles may be changing, but the world-view shaped by the revolution lives on in the mainstream of our culture—in our schools, our businesses, our inner cities. In the next chapters we'll look at what this means for our society as a whole and, more directly, how it affects the way we work.

PART 3

The Predatory Society

I'll never forget walking through the South Bronx
. . . and seeing boys, thirteen or fourteen years old,
wearing these necklaces with silvery rings hanging from
them. . . . I thought these were peace symbols.
. . . Of course, when I looked more closely, I saw they
were Mercedes-Benz hood ornaments. These boys knew
what a Mercedes-Benz was, and they knew how much it
cost because they knew that all the hotshots drive them.
The drug dealers drive them. They wanted theirs. And
they were taking the only part that they could now get,
which was the hood ornament. This was the money fever spreading right down to the bottom rungs of the
social ladder. This is New York. And this is vanity, operating on all sides.

Tom Wolfe[1]

5

The Society That Preys Together

A new breed of Americans born out of the social movements of the 60s and grown into a majority in the 70s, holds a set of values so markedly different from the traditional outlook that they promise to transform the character of work in America in the 80s.

Daniel Yankelovitch[2]

AN HONEST DAY'S WORK FOR AN honest day's pay." Almost every American over forty recalls hearing or being taught this axiom. For generations it was passed from parent to child, drilled into young people along with the multiplication tables. Today the expression sounds so quaint that it becomes a punch line able to draw mocking laughter on national television.

Comedian Jay Leno, in a special on the American dream, visits an efficient and successful American auto plant. Except the cars it manufactures are toys.

People laugh.

A character dressed up as Uncle Sam can't linger for an interview because he's on his way to open up a new Toyota dealership.

More laughter.

The popular comic then takes us to a club where he asks a member of the audience for her concept of the American dream.

"Make a lot of money," she replies without hesitation. The audience murmurs approval.

"And how do you get that money?" asks Leno.

"Beg, borrow, or steal," she replies.

"Of course, any kind of work would be foolish," Leno shoots back. An honest day's work for an honest day's pay! How hopelessly naive.

No, the rebellion of the sixties did not end with our withdrawal from Vietnam or the great catharsis known as Watergate. The children of Aquarius merely shaved their beards, traded in their ragged jeans and baggy dresses for three-piece suits, and marched off into the workplace toting their revolutionary new view of the world.

Existentialism teaches that since life is meaningless, we have two choices. Either we make an heroic effort to overcome the nothingness, or we pursue meaningless pleasure and gratify our senses. This world-view translated itself in several ways in the 1970s and 1980s.

Those who believed that life consisted of gratifying the senses did grow up; their pleasures just became more expensive.

Thus, the yuppies were not an aberration. Their behavior was perfectly consistent with the philosophy of the revolution—their work became simply a means to an end. The more one worked, the more ends there were to enjoy. The aim was not producing goods for others or for the common welfare but acquiring things for one's own pleasure. "He who dies with the most toys, wins," proclaimed the quintessential yuppie bumper sticker on the BMWs that transported hedonism from Woodstock to Madison Avenue. There the disciples of the sixties now worked feverishly to pay for their

Ralph Lauren labels and their Dom Perignon wines.

Not surprisingly, one of the great growth industries of the seventies and eighties was leisure. Marketers found more and more ways to relieve people of their money by giving them what they thought they wanted—vacation homes, sports cars, games and toys. (At least creativity didn't die!)

Now we don't mean to argue against leisure; after all, God created rest as well as workweeks. But don't things seem a bit out of kilter when universities tenure "professors of leisure" (one of whom was recently fired for practicing too much of what he taught)[3] and scholars write "serious" books and articles promoting the virtues of idleness and attacking the "achievement society"?[4]

Meanwhile, those who were not kept busy pursuing leisure for its own sake were determined to overcome the nothingness of life by their own heroic efforts. In the eighties this led to the equally pernicious extreme of working for work's sake.

Men like Ivan Boesky became the ultimate existentialists, proving that in an empty, meaningless universe you can build a posh world for yourself—if, of course, you are willing to live off the work of others and ignore such quaint notions as right and wrong. And the Michael Milkens became workaholics with little regard for enjoying the benefits of their labors.

Generally portrayed in the media as a scheming, sinister character who manipulated the market, Milken may be better understood as the all-American dream come true, eighties style. Born on the fourth of July, he worked as a young man helping his accountant father. He was a good student at Berkeley, he neither smoked nor drank, he married his childhood sweetheart, and, if friends are to be believed, remained faithful through the years.

His work habits became legend: his sixteen- to twenty-hour workdays began at 4:30 A.M., and Milken boasted that he ate his lunch at his desk in five minutes or less. Yet friends claimed that it wasn't greed that drove him. Milken was anything but greedy, they said; what he really cared about was raising money for small, worthy companies in need.

Greedy or not, he became incredibly rich. From the $100 billion dollars he sold in junk bonds, Milken made over $1 billion for himself. Yet he lived moderately, at least by billionaire standards; he gave away well over $300 million to foundations to help the poor; and many reported that he seemed happiest when he was helping crippled children.[5]

But with no transcendent values, and no goal other than pleasure or work for work's sake, traditional restraints on behavior collapsed. Thus was born a new breed of predators who exploited everything for their own advantage, making exceptions for themselves instead of playing by the rules. And why not? There were few rules. In the distribution of worldly rewards, raw ambition counted more heavily than laws or morality. Ivan Boesky expressed this eighties ethic succinctly when he told a group of Berkeley students that "greed is healthy."[6] Acquiring money, as much as possible in any way possible, is what counts.

Actor Michael Douglas, playing the unscrupulous corporate raider in Oliver Stone's movie *Wall Street,* put it even more forcefully. Grabbing the lapels of the naive rookie broker, played by Charlie Sheen, Douglas screams, "Somebody wins and somebody loses. Money isn't gained, it's transferred. I create nothing."

No one is a better or more perceptive critic of contemporary culture than author Tom Wolfe, who chronicled the eighties in his novel *Bonfire of the Vanities.* The central character is Wall Street bond trader Sherman McCoy, a patrician Yale graduate who lives in a New York apartment he purchased for $2.6 million with a $1.8 million mortgage. His monthly payment is $21,000, which he barely manages on his million-dollar-a-year salary.

Sherman reflects that if his father, a lawyer, ever found out, he would be wounded at the thought of "how his endlessly repeated lessons concerning duty, debt, ostentation, and proportion had whistled straight through his son's skull."

At one point, Sherman's six-year-old daughter, Campbell, asks him, "Daddy . . . what do you do?" Sherman cannot produce a quick answer. His daughter's friend's father publishes books—that's easy enough to explain. But bond dealing? While he thinks about it, Sherman's father agrees that the question is excellent, and surely speaks for most Americans when he wonders aloud, "I've often asked myself what it is you fellows do, exactly."

"What are bonds? What is deal?" presses Campbell.

Sherman explains that while he doesn't build roads or hospitals, and doesn't even help build them, he does "handle the bonds for the people who raise the money."

This doesn't satisfy the young inquisitor, and Sherman's wife Judy, who is disillusioned with her husband—whom she suspects, correctly, of infidelity—intervenes. A bond is like a slice of cake, she says, "and every time you hand someone a slice of cake, a tiny little bit comes off, like a little crumb, and you can keep that." And "pretty soon you have enough crumbs to make a gigantic cake."[7]

Sherman squirms miserably, but the arrow flies straight to the heart. Certainly, there is a need for and a value in honest brokerage. Money managers and lenders deserve commissions for their work—it is a neccessary part of our economy. But, like so many in the eighties, Sherman was oblivious to anything other than supporting his high-flying lifestyle and was unable even to justify his work to his daughter.

Much of the Wall Street boom, as Judy put it so graphically, was like scooping up crumbs from the cake—expensive golden crumbs. Money earned without regard to the value of the goods or services provided or to the general welfare of society can lead to parasitism. Not much different really from the Communist party hack we observed in the Moscow airport lounge.

Many excesses in the eighties were caused by government's guarantee to individual investors against large losses in banks and S&Ls and by not controlling mergers and acquisitions that generated the junk bonds. Some banks, insurance companies, and

S&Ls got rich on paper only, while individuals, like Sherman McCoy, were enticed into living beyond their means.

For decades S&Ls were the conservative, hometown financial institutions run by stodgy men in starched white shirts and conservative ties. They took depositors' money, paid market interest rates, and loaned it out at a modest profit for safe homeowner mortgages. It was a good, solid, feet-on-the-ground business.

Then came the eighties and many S&Ls started to fly high. Government guarantees on deposits were increased to $100,000; restraints on investments were lifted; interest rates soared and money flooded in. Many S&Ls turned away from solid ventures like neighborhood home mortgages and plunged into speculations and high-yielding commercial real estate deals or junk bonds. This produced huge paper profits, which in turn supported the most extravagant indulgences of some of the owners and operators—jet planes, multi-million-dollar art collections, expensive wine, and even more expensive women.

The S&L operators also managed to stuff bundles of cash into the campaign coffers of senators and congressmen who in turn pressured regulators to look the other way.

The junk bonds the S&Ls purchased were supplied by the machinations of greedy business and financial institutions. For their labors, the Wall Street stars were handsomely paid, and many became the new American heroes.

When Milken was indicted, his employees and friends crowded the courtroom to cheer him. He'd accomplished what really mattered—he'd made money for himself and for them. Like a grand game of cheaters' Monopoly, it didn't matter how many rules were broken on the way to the bank; all that mattered was cash. "How much" was the measure of success.

But with all restraints released, people don't just take what they need; they grab whatever they can get—before someone else does. On the streets it's called looting, and during the heyday of the acquisitive eighties a looter's mentality infected commerce.

Fraud and breach of fiduciary duty went wild with insider trading, personal use of corporate funds, backroom deals, and reciprocal arrangements.

When the inevitable day of reckoning arrived, Wall Street firms went bankrupt, the S&L industry was ravaged, and the tax-payers were left holding a $550-billion bag. And some, like Ivan Boesky and Michael Milkin, finally landed on Go to Jail.

But when this win-regardless-of-the-cost mentality invades the workplace, the consequences can be even more disastrous than prison.

Roger Boisjoly was a senior engineer with Morton Thiokol, the company that manufactured the boosters and the rubber O-rings that sealed the joint between the boosters and the fuel tanks on NASA's space shuttles. An expert on rocket seals, Boisjoly was carefully monitoring O-ring malfunctions at low temperatures; he warned NASA and Thiokol against any launch when temperatures dropped below 53 degrees.

On January 27, 1986, the night before the *Challenger* launch, the weather bureau predicted a morning temperature of 18 degrees; Morton Thiokol's managers recommended the launch be scrubbed. But under pressure from NASA, the senior vice president decided to "take off his engineer's cap and put on his management cap."[8]

Previously Boisjoly had to prove that the flight was safe before the launch would be approved. Now management turned the tables. Boisjoly would have to prove that the seal would malfunction. Management called Boisjoly's evidence "inconclusive" and approved the launch.

That night Boisjoly wrote in his journal: "I sincerely hope that this launch does not result in a catastrophe."[9]

The next morning as Boisjoly stood in the chilly air watching the *Challenger* arc through the sky sixty seconds into its flight, he breathed a prayer of thanks. Thirteen seconds later the enormous pressure of gases from the boosters blew past the rubber O-ring, still stiff with cold. The *Challenger* exploded in mid-air.[10]

The company's decision to approve the launch was apparently bottom-line: NASA was the client, NASA paid the bills, and NASA was tired of waiting. And when the bottom line is balanced against lives in a predatory society, it is often the bottom line that wins.

The Beech-Nut Apple Juice scandal is a less dramatic, but no less sinister example. For generations of mothers, Beech-Nut baby foods have been a symbol of health and purity. Then federal agents realized they had a bad apple on their hands: the product the company had sold for ten years as apple juice ("100% fruit juice—no sugar added") was not much more than chemicals, dye, and water.

Did Beech-Nut dump the "fraudulent chemical cocktail," as one company chemist described it? Well, yes, in a manner of speaking.

Beech-Nut had employees work all night to load nine tractor trailers with the stuff, and within days the juice was being sold to trusting mothers in Puerto Rico, the Dominican Republic, and the Virgin Islands.[11]

Beech-Nut played the game for profit, winner take all.

The looter mentality may not always be quite so obvious, but it has permeated every level of the work force.

For instance, propped up on the check-in counter of a Mobile, Alabama, hotel frequented by business travelers, a large sign reads "Rooms $80; Cash rebate $20." The message is thinly disguised but clear: check in here, charge your employer eighty dollars on your expense account, and we'll put twenty dollars in your pocket.

Then there's the young businessman, a churchgoer from a solid family, who told us he regularly "looks the other way" when his boss takes home company equipment for moonlighting jobs. The boss in turn is very generous with our young friend, who seemed genuinely surprised when we challenged him on this. "That's business, isn't it? Everybody does it," he shrugged.

"Everybody does it" is the rationalization that has caused us to accept and then institutionalize corruption.

The government has not been immune from this looters' mentality. In the past decade we have tripled our national debt to $3 trillion, saddling our children with debt for years to come. Nothing could be more profound proof of the death of the work ethic in America and the reckless abandonment of one of its most cherished traditions—thrift.

These attitudes bred in the revolution have not only created an ethical malaise among jet-setting business leaders, they have also sapped the meaning from work for the average wage earner.

A 1980 Gallup poll conducted for the Chamber of Commerce found that people still believed in work ethic values: 88 percent said working hard and doing their best on the job was personally important. But were they doing that?

In a 1982 survey for a nonprofit foundation, workers were asked that very question. Only 16 percent said they were doing the best job they could at work; 84 percent said they could be working harder and doing better. Many said they could be twice as effective.

Working hard was personally important, but they weren't doing it.

Why the astounding dichotomy? Because, said 84 percent, they would work harder if they gained something from it.[12]

This "what's in it for me" cynicism is a direct consequence of the sixties rejection of transcendent values—the idea that there is something worth living or working for beyond ourselves. Psychologist Robert Bellah calls this "radical individualism."

Surveying two hundred middle-class Americans, the eminent UCLA professor discovered that people seek *personal* advancement from work, *personal* development from marriage, and *personal* fulfillment from church. Everything—their perspective on family, church, community, and work—was utilitarian; it was measured by what they could get out of it. Concern for others was secondary.[13]

James Sheehy, an executive with a computer firm, saw first-hand how this was affecting the workplace. He wanted a better understanding of the expectations and psyche of younger employees, so he spent his two-week vacation working in a fast-food restaurant. Most of his coworkers were from upper-income families; they did not *need* to work, but wanted extra spending money.

Sheehy watched and listened as his coworkers displayed poor work habits and contempt for customers. His conclusion? We have a new generation of workers whose "habits and experiences will plague future employers for years."

Along with their get-away-with-what-you-can attitude and indifference to the quality of performance, their basic work ethic "was dominated by a type of gamesmanship that revolved around taking out of the system or milking the place dry." Theft, skimming, and baiting management were rampant, and skill levels "surprisingly low." The workers saw long hours and hard work as counterproductive. "You only put in time for the big score," one said.

After recounting his experience, Sheehy concluded: "Get ready, America. There's more of this to come from the work force of tomorrow."[14]

Perhaps the most alarming fallout from all this is the fact that not only does much of the populace not understand or recognize what went wrong; they no longer even have the language to discuss the ethical issues that plague us. Chuck encountered this reality when he was invited to give a lecture at Harvard Business School.

In the wake of the Wall Street and S&L scandals, the business school established a new ethics course, and the university invited Chuck to address the student body on the subject "Why Good People Do Bad Things."

Never one to mince words, Chuck told the students that Harvard could never teach business ethics because it did not believe in absolute values. The best it could do would be to teach pragmatic business judgments.

"You can't teach ethics here because you don't believe there are moral laws," he said. "But there are moral laws just as certain as there are physical laws. We are simply unwilling to admit it because it interferes with our desire to do whatever we please, and doing what we please has become the supreme virtue of our society. Places like Harvard, indeed Harvard of all institutions, propagate these kinds of values."

Chuck expected some sort of response from his audience—Harvard students have a reputation for hissing at speakers who displease them. But his speech was met with passive silence followed by polite applause. During the question-and-answer period that followed, students politely asked questions that had almost nothing to do with ethics, and not one student challenged his thesis.

Chuck was puzzled. Later he called the organizers of the event. "Why such a docile response?" he asked.

"The material you presented was totally new to them," said one young man. "They didn't have the tools to debate it."

These students were too absorbed in getting their MBAs and their $70,000-a-year starting salaries to take time for debate. Furthermore, they couldn't have debated if they'd wanted to: they didn't have the language or the insight to mount an argument.

That's chilling. Because these students are going to be our next Savings and Loan officers, the next CEOs of our major corporations, our next senators and legislators. And they have absolutely no ethical foundation for the work they will be doing.

It's not surprising. After all, today's college students are the products of an educational system that is in deep trouble.

6

A Nation at Risk

Imagine an industry that consistently fails to do what it sets out to do, a factory where this year's product is invariably sleazier than last year's but, nevertheless, better than next year's. Imagine a corporation whose executives are always spending vast sums of money on studies designed to discover just what it is they are supposed to do and then vaster sums for further studies on just how to do it. Imagine a plant devoted to the manufacture of factory seconds to be sold at a loss. Imagine a producer of vacuum cleaners that rarely work hiring whole platoons of engineers who will, in time, report that it is in fact true that the vacuum cleaners rarely work, and who will, for a larger fee, be glad to find out why, if that's possible. If you discover some such outfit, don't invest in it. Unfortunately, we are all required to invest in public education.

Richard Mitchell[1]

DID YOU KNOW THAT THE HOLOCAUST was a Jewish holiday? That's what a majority of high school students told ABC interviewers preparing for a Barbara Walters special on the deterioration of American education. Among the same group, many could not locate the United States on a world map.

Professors Diane Ravitch and Chester Finn, who conducted a survey of high school students in 1986, discovered that 31.9 percent did not know that Columbus reached the New World before 1750; 30 percent could not place the Civil War in the proper half century; 52.7 percent had "heard of" President Kennedy's famous "ask not" dictum, but 29.2 percent attributed it to Teddy Roosevelt; 15 percent thought Joe McCarthy was a civil-rights advocate for the Irish, and 29.4 identified him as a protester of American involvement in Vietnam.[2]

In 1945 the vocabulary of American children aged six to fourteen was twenty-five thousand words. By 1990 it had dropped to ten thousand words.[3]

American students finished dead last in a 1988 competition in math.[4] In chemistry and physics American students lag behind nearly all countries, and in biology they rank last, behind even Singapore and Thailand, countries many Americans regard as backward.[5]

This decline in knowledge is also evident in the college Scholastic Aptitude Tests. In 1914 potential college students were asked to do such things as compare Themistocles and Aristides as to statesmanship and character, to calculate the amount of silver chloride that may be precipitated by silver nitrate from one kilogram of sea water containing 2.5 percent sodium chloride, and to translate a Latin passage.[6]

Granted, only the academic elite took the test eighty years ago, but today even our college graduates would be hard-pressed to pass that 1914 exam. At Harvard, where we are led to believe the best and the brightest study, one junior recently thought Toronto was in Italy; a senior sat through a commencement address by King Juan Carlos without knowing that the speaker was the king of Spain; and one student took a course in Latin because she thought it was the language spoken in Latin America.[7]

Extreme examples? Perhaps. But indicative nonetheless of an alarming pattern.

When it comes to those high school graduates headed directly for the job market, many are functionally illiterate, incapable of even filling out a job application form. Industries are having to set up company-sponsored programs to complete the most basic educational needs of their employees.

In the early 1980s the federal government appointed a National Commission on Excellence in Education, which published its findings in 1983 under the alarming title *A Nation at Risk*. The commission concluded that the educational foundation of our society is being eroded by "a rising tide of mediocrity that threatens our very future as a nation and a people."[8]

The revolution strikes again!

With the removal of prayer from the classroom and the purging of America's religious history and heritage from school textbooks,[9] education has been "freed" from the "oppressive" influences of the Judeo-Christian tradition. Unfortunately individual accountability, personal achievement, and the work ethic fall squarely within that tradition.

Despite the fact that for nearly twenty-three hundred years educators in Western civilization held fast to Plato's view that the purpose of education was to make good people because good people would behave nobly, in the sixties our school systems began a wholesale effort to abandon any teaching that reflected moral values. Education, that had for centuries formed character along with imparting knowledge, now became a "value-free" instrument of social therapy and experimentation that institutionalized the freewheeling lifestyle of the sixties. Sidney Simon of the University of Massachusetts, chief promoter of the ubiquitous "values clarification," believed that teaching values to children was a form of brainwashing.

Yet consider what "values clarification" really means. California, Virginia, and several other states have in recent years introduced this kind of curriculum. Virginia's is called "Family Life

Education," a twelve-year curriculum which, among other things, teaches eighth-grade students that if they are confused by their attraction to students of the same sex, they should simply adjust their values to accommodate this desire. A tenth-grade course lists "experiencing sexual intimacy" and "getting wheels" as critical normative events in the process of becoming an independent person at sixteen.[10]

Leaving aside the sexual teaching, which is anything but value neutral, what does it say to a sixteen-year-old that having a car is an essential part of the process of growing up? The course teaches nothing about working for the car. It conveys only one message: put pressure on your parents for your "rights." When less affluent families can't afford to provide this "right," the sixteen-year-old feels resentful and left out of what he or she perceives as an essential process of maturity. Little wonder teenagers struggle to maintain their self-esteem! And little wonder that they grow up seeing things like cars and toys as "rights" rather than something to be earned by working for them. Thus the work ethic has given way to an ethic of entitlement.

It's not just morality that has been cut out of the culture; it seems that values clarification dispenses with common decency as well. Illustrative was a session in a Teaneck, New Jersey, high school observed by a *New York Times* reporter. When a group of students were asked their opinions on the conduct of a young woman who found $1,000 and turned it in, all fifteen students said she was a fool.

After the class the stunned reporter asked the teacher why he hadn't offered his opinion on the matter; that is, why hadn't he told the students they were wrong?

The educator's reply?

"If I came from the position of what is right and wrong, then I'm not their counselor."

Although this attitude strikes us as almost criminally apathetic, it is totally consistent with the ethos of the revolution. Some teachers see themselves as counselors rather than educators, wasting valuable classtime on amateur pschotherapy rather than the three R's.

Passed through this emptiness masquerading as ideology, thousands of schoolchildren emerged intellectually and morally crippled for life.

When the revolution battle lines were drawn against values, other qualities suffered from the assault—like personal account-ability and achievement. After all, if pleasure is the only reason-able goal in a life without transcendent meaning, what is there to strive for? What is there to achieve? Or why care about the common good?

As a result of this, the attitudes of students, even subcon-sciously, are affected. They simply no longer work as hard or, evi-dence shows, as long.

American children go to school for an average of 180 days per year—a little less than half a year; in Europe and Japan the school year runs well over 200 days. By the time they finish high school, the European and Japanese students are several years ahead of their American counterparts. In fact, many European high school stu-dents know as much at graduation as their American counterparts with bachelor degrees from state colleges.[11] Would they learn that much more in an extra twenty or thirty days a year? It's hard to say. But lengthy vacations and short school days do send students the wrong message: real life begins after school; therefore, spend as little time on schoolwork as possible.

American students are learning less than their parents did and less than their peers in other countries. Instead, they are often be-ing taught that accepting homosexuality is more important than learning the three R's.

One would expect an angry response from a country that is eagerly awaiting the next generation of citizens to enter the work force. One might also expect to hear an outcry for more testing, more homework, better teachers.

But anyone who expects those things has forgotten what cen-tury we're living in. Another legacy of the sixties is a refusal to acknowledge any standards. Personal fulfillment and therapy have become the goals, while measurements or standards of excellence are viewed as oppressive and anti-egalitarian. This has infected the whole world of education.

If today's students don't measure up, perhaps it's because many of their teachers don't either.

Certainly, there are many great educators in both public and private schools, both in the inner city and in the suburbs. But their pursuit of excellence is the exception—the system makes few demands on them.

For example, in twenty-six states, competency tests for teachers require only minimum standards. Answering 47 out of 104 questions correctly is considered a passing grade, even though no self-respecting teacher would pass a student who answered less than 50 percent of the questions on an exam correctly. The state of Georgia allows its educators to take the state licensing test nine times. In California a full 31 percent of new teachers failed the state's Basic Education Skills test in one year; a test which, as the president of the California Teachers' Association said, "any competent high-school student should be able to pass."[12] The math questions on the test involved knowing how to find the perimeter of a figure and the reading section asked the teachers to find the "main idea" in a 200-word paragraph.

Little wonder that educators resist standards that would hold them or their students accountable. In fact, the educational establishment seems to be moving in exactly the opposite direction by advocating "open education" that would chuck tests, report cards, and even grades because they violate what seems to be a new commandment for educators: "Thou shalt not make any student feel inferior."

Ideas such as "holistic grading" assess the students' compositions not on organization, punctuation, diction, and spelling, but on "its total impression of quality." Educational critic Richard Mitchell comments that this is like judging a musical composition without reference to rhythm, tempo, or notes, and wonders whether the radical educationists would want the work of their doctors and electricians rated on this "holistic" scale.

It is no longer enough to line everyone up in the same place at the same starting line and give them the same advantages; everyone has to cross the finish line at the same time as well. As Dodo gushed after the race in *Alice in Wonderland*, "*Everybody* has won and we all must have prizes."

As Richard Cohen notes: "The penchant to praise and to build self-esteem has produced an academic culture that values the little smile sticker on a test paper more than knowledge itself. It's not what you know that counts, it's how you feel about it."[13]

Any objective observer also has to be struck by the extraordinary inefficiencies of our present educational system. During the same period in which we have witnessed a frightening decline in achievement, we have also seen the number of personnel involved in education increase dramatically. From 1960 to 1984 the number of teachers grew by 57 percent but the number of principals and supervisors increased by 79 percent. Overall, the number of nonteaching staffers shot up by nearly 500 percent.[14] At present, for every 100 teachers in California there are 106 "nonteaching" employees.[15] Former Education Secretary William Bennett called this expensive bureaucratic quagmire "the blob." Robert Sarrel, a budget director for the New York City Board of Education's high school division, decided to track every dollar of the $1.4 billion spent on New York City high school students in 1988-89. He found that the city spent $6,107 per high school student, well above the national average, but nonclassroom services ate up an astounding $4,135 of that amount. [16] One liberal columnist described this as "grand theft pedagogy."[17]

In the midst of all this, one factor has remained constant. The educational establishment, especially teachers' unions like the National Education Association, beats the drum for more money. If it's broke, throw money at it.

But former Education Secretary Lauro Cavazos acknowledged that "we are already spending more money per student than our major foreign competitors, Japan and Germany," and yet, "our students consistently fall behind the competition in competitive testing. . . . Money alone is not the answer to our education deficit."[18]

The evidence bears this out. After the Great Society of the sixties opened the federal financial floodgates, spending for education *tripled* between 1964 and 1976—the very same period that saw the sharpest losses in student productivity and achievement.[19] Spending per student rose from $3,165 in 1982 to $3,977 in 1987, a 26 percent increase during a time of low inflation. In 1989, national per-pupil expenditures came to $4,800, about $1,500 higher than when *A Nation at Risk* was released and higher than any country in the world with the possible exception of Switzerland.[20] And still we are failing to prepare students to be productive members of our community.

When *A Nation at Risk* was published in 1983, 6 million copies of the report were distributed in one year. "Excellence" became a buzzword. Reformers rolled up their sleeves. Alarm bells sounded in classrooms across the country. Despite all the furor, talk, and money, however, we've made little real progress toward educational excellence.

By the year 2000, the Brock report reveals, 70 percent of the jobs in America will not require a college education. These jobs are the mainstay of our economy, and the productivity of workers in these positions will make or break our economic future.

Yet the evidence is that we have shortchanged vocational education. Rather than providing quality education and training for this vast army, we have neglected the needs of vocational students and developed a caste system that measures high schools by the percentage of their students who go on to college and that invests most of its creative energy into college-prep programs.

Education is not a luxury reserved for the academic elite. It is a right and necessity for every citizen.

Right now some 25 percent of students drop out of high school, with the figure climbing to 50 percent in poor and minority areas.[21] And 52 percent of those dropouts are either unemployed or on welfare.[22]

If we don't start training our next generation of workers and citizens now, we may never get the chance.

7

A Generation Condemned

America doesn't have just one economy—we have in reality, two economies, separate and unequal. . . . Our
second economy—the welfare economy—is more akin to
the Third World socialist economy than to the capitalist
west. It is a grim world in which the rules of the market
are reversed by government fiat, and where there is too
little private property and too much publicly owned and
managed property.

Jack Kemp[1]

On the gray streets of Moscow we saw some of the most dejected, dispirited expressions we'd encountered anywhere in the
world. Sadly, though, you can find the same closer to home. Just
walk the streets of New York or Los Angeles or Dallas.

Or Chicago.

Columnist George Will describes a housing project called
Cabrini Green, a landscape of gang graffiti, drug deals, and sudden
violence, where the residents have been turned into inmates, afraid

to venture outside into what has become a kind of free-fire zone. Inside, the children sleep five and six to a bed, stacked like cordwood on piled-up mattresses. Some go to school smelling of urine because it is too cold for the younger ones to get up and go to the bathroom.

Meanwhile, the local school system has been called "institutionalized child-neglect" where first graders do not know their numbers or colors, and sixth graders do not know how many inches are in a foot. They have never used a ruler.

Will calls the scene at the Chicago project a "panorama of pain, waste and the perpetuation of squalor," a "chilling example of rebarbarization." In Cabrini Green he saw a world where life is "poor, nasty, brutish and short."[2]

But wasn't it that very brutishness that the government's most ambitious programs of the sixties were supposed to cure? Wasn't this the Great Society's vision, proclaimed in the revolution's moment of triumphant glory? Since God was dead, was not the state his logical heir?

What has happened in Cabrini Green and elsewhere is a direct result of good intentions turned sour. The idea that took root during the revolution—that man was his own master destined to make the "inhumane humane"—led naturally to a form of political utopianism. By our own superior knowledge and effort and money we could create a perfect society.

The war on poverty in America began with infectious optimism. President John Kennedy, in a 1962 address to Congress, called for the creation of a "public welfare program" designed to "attack dependency, juvenile delinquency, family breakdown, illegitimacy, ill health and disability." His successor, Lyndon Johnson, assembled a new "Marshal Plan" to eradicate poverty, and in 1964 his *Economic Report of the President* claimed, "Conquest of poverty is well within our power."[3]

Johnson's promise of a Great Society was no empty political rhetoric; he was a thoroughgoing utopian, convinced that with enough money and resources, poverty could be eliminated, cities transformed, and full employment achieved. But like most utopian schemes, the war on poverty had precisely the reverse effect: it institutionalized a perverse incentive structure that penalized work and self-improvement, and it defined the poor as victims of the capitalistic system, racism, and deprivation.

The Great Society was a disaster, according to one eminent scholar, not so much because of its ineffective programs as because of the emphasis on welfare as "entitlement" rather than need.[4] Before long, welfare hearings became legal circuses where the poor were treated like zoo animals at feeding time, instead of women and men created with moral responsibilities. And the more time the victims of this process spent on the dole, the more their work skills deteriorated.

This same process took place in inner-city schools. Ironically the Jim Crow system of segregation was finally being eliminated, only to be replaced with a more insidious form of racism: the notion that minorities could not and should not be expected to work as hard or perform as well as their white counterparts. Thus a generation got slammed from both sides. School programs in the inner cities were geared down to the lowest common denominator even as the welfare system enforced the egalitarianism of mediocrity and failure.

As a result of all this, the Great Society became more of a declaration of war on the work ethic than on poverty. Between the mid-1940s and the mid-1960s, poverty rates had been cut in half. Suddenly this went into reverse. With our tax dollars at work, poverty among working-age Americans began to rise and the underclass began to take shape. Today, that underclass is trapped in a culture that teaches them not to work and not to hope for better than they have.

Much of this underclass is black, which has led some to believe that these problems are somehow rooted in the history or makeup of the black community. Nothing could be further from the truth. The black community in America has a rich tradition of family and work.

A 1905 survey of fifteen thousand black families in New York found just one woman heading a single-parent family with more than two children. "The two-parent nuclear family remained the predominant type for both blacks and whites up to World War II," argues sociologist William Julius Wilson.[5] Yet today in some inner city communities 90 percent of the children are born into fatherless homes.

And the black community once enjoyed a powerful work ethic. "Although it is difficult to remember now," writes William Tucker, "one of the major social stigmas attached to blacks in the 1930s was not that they 'wouldn't work' but that they were *too willing* to work. As late as 1948, black teenage unemployment was actually lower than white teenage unemployment."[6] A 1910 study found that 71 percent of blacks of employable age had jobs while the white rate was only 51 percent.[7] Blacks were resented by unions because they were considered "cheap labor," willing to work longer for less pay. In the 1950s blacks and whites participated in the labor force at about the same rate.

Millions of men and women whose parents, grandparents, and great-grandparents managed to survive centuries of war, dislocation, slavery, oppression, and poverty have had generations of traditional values and habits destroyed during a few decades of what should have been increasing stability and peace.

This process has not been cheap. Since the 1960s, the government has plowed trillions into welfare programs, and the administration of these programs has become a huge industry in itself. At present it takes more than 5 million well-paid government employees to deliver $109 billion yearly to some 42 million working-age women and their children. Clearly, one segment of society is benefiting from the failed programs, but it's not those caught in the poverty trap.[8]

The real failure is not the government's generosity, but its approach. George Gilder, social critic and author of *Wealth and Poverty*, vividly describes the process that fuels this problem.

A fifteen-year-old in the ghetto is doing poorly at school,

fighting with her mother, and afraid of men in the house. She wants to escape, and when she turns sixteen, the government offers her a chance for independence. She can get her own apartment, medicine, legal aid, and a combination of welfare payments and food stamps. But there's a catch. To get these benefits, she must bear an illegitimate child, and she must not work.

"In the face of such an overwhelming inducement from the state," says Gilder, "illegitimacy is no longer penalized and thus comes to be seen as an acceptable form of behavior." Little wonder that "millions of young women have launched children into the welfare culture."[9]

The result is Aid to Families with Dependent Children, which has created a permanently subsidized class with built-in disincentives for family and work—at huge cost to taxpayers. Some 5 million young women who bear illegitimate children are paid a monthly sum *provided* they do not work and do not get married.

But what is even more frightening is that this process is self-perpetuating. The breakdown in family life has an immediate effect on the children, since it is in families that human beings learn manners, hygiene, speech, discipline, morality, values, and the importance of getting and holding a job. Once the cycle of dependency has begun, each generation sinks deeper into despair and hopelessness. It is difficult to break and nearly impossible to escape.

This has been termed the "moral hazard effect."

Katie Brown, a young black girl living in Florida, got pregnant when she was in the tenth grade. She entered a forced marriage with an alcoholic who beat her. Then she started using drugs. She divorced her husband and met a new boyfriend, but he also abused her. Katie turned to crack. To pay for her habit, she turned to prostitution. But drugs weren't the only habit she found hard to kick.

"Welfare and food stamps can be like a drug," she says. "You start using, you get addicted, you don't want to work." After thirty-three years on welfare, Katie has now managed to escape and recover. Many others have not.[10]

Along with the moral hazard effect, dependency has a long-term economic effect. Economists call it a "skill-depreciation effect." As individuals spend more time on welfare and less time in the work force, their skills depreciate and their work record deteriorates. These men and women, in turn, raise children who never even develop the skills needed to escape from poverty.[11]

What is most alarming, however, is the psychology of victimization fostered by the welfare system. "Your condition is not your fault. You are not responsible," it says. "You are victims of economic forces and discrimination. Society is to blame for your plight." This is the voice of the revolution, the utopian philosophy that refuses to assign individual blame or responsibility.

On the surface this may sound like compassion. In practice and reality it is a dehumanizing process that destroys both individual responsibility and dignity. To treat disadvantaged men and women as victims rather than morally responsible individuals only reinforces an expectation of failure—an expectation too often fulfilled.

America, like other countries, has always had a certain amount of poverty. Previous generations knew economic need, disease, and even squalor. But no generation of the poor has known this kind of utter hopelessness and isolation. These poor are part of something unprecedented: a class of people who not only struggle against economic need, but are imprisoned within an environment permeated with profoundly self-destructive behavior.

The only ones who escape end up in another kind of prison. The kind with bars.

At the height of the sixties triumphalism, LBJ's Attorney General Ramsey Clark declared, "Poverty is the cause of crime." Crime wasn't the result of individual sin or wrong moral choices. The criminals were not to blame. It was all society's fault.

The result? A crime wave in America's cities unprecedented in history. Soon we were chalking up the highest murder rate in the world. Today 25 percent of the black inner-city males aged nineteen to thirty-one—those the Great Society set out to protect from the consequences of their own behavior—are in prison or on parole, where they become members of an enforced culture of indolence.

America may trail Japan and Germany in automobiles, but there is one area in which we are clearly number one: our rate of incarceration.

Just a few years ago the United States was third behind the Soviet Union and South Africa in the percentage of population in prison. That was bad enough. But in the last two years the prison populations in both those countries have declined while ours has skyrocketed.

In the 1980s America's prison population doubled; since 1970 it has tripled. That means our prison population is growing ten times faster than our population in general. Nearly a million men, women, and young people are behind bars.

Any who still believe that prisons deter crime need only look at the crime statistics of the 1980s. During the same period that saw the incredible prison population boom, crime consistently rose. In 1990 alone, violent crime rose 10 percent, and over twenty thousand people were slaughtered on the mean streets of our nation. During the hundred hours in which the air and ground warfare of Desert Storm bombarded Iraq, more Americans died on the city streets of their own country than in the sands of the Middle East.

The cost of all this is absolutely staggering. During the last decade, California added thirty thousand prison beds at a cost of nearly $4 billion and still ended up ten thousand beds short. The operating budget for California's prison system is $2.3 billion. That's more than the gross national product of many smaller nations—and a major cause of California's 1991 tax increase.

According to Department of Justice statistics, it costs $80,000 to build a maximum security cell and almost $16,000 a year to keep someone in it for a year, which is more than the annual tuition at some of our better universities.

Now don't misunderstand. We need prisons. Dangerous criminals must be locked up and separated from society. But half the people in prison are there for nonviolent, nondangerous offenses and are being punished in ways that are neither productive nor life-changing. Some 74 percent of those released are re-arrested within four years, generally on more serious charges.

It's bad enough that our prisons are not working. But neither are the prisoners.

Between the two of us, we have visited more than four hundred prisons in America, and in every one we have seen men and women lying on their bunks staring at the ceiling with nothing to do. We've walked the cell blocks where inmates live in six-by-nine cages with tiny black-and-white television sets, a few books—and absolutely nothing to do. We've seen the sullen expressions, the downcast eyes, the simmering bitterness.

The world's most brilliant behavioral scientist could not design a more destructive system than to lock a person in a cell, give him or her nothing to do for years on end, and then loose them back on society.

This is a relatively new development in America. When the prison system began two centuries ago, inmates paid for their confinement with honest, productive labor. In 1828 approximately 85 percent of the inmates were gainfully employed. But by the turn of the century, the protests had begun. "Unfair competition," argued business and labor leaders in the rapidly industrializing environment. They got reaction from the top when President Teddy Roosevelt banned the federal government from purchasing prison-made goods. (Fortunately, this law was later reversed.) In the mid-1930s and again in the late 1940s additional statutes were passed banning the sale of some prison-made goods in interstate commerce. This effectively killed any connection between prison industry and the free market.

By 1940 only 44 percent of inmates were working, and it has been steadily downhill ever since. By 1990 less than 10 percent of our nation's inmates were working in prison industries.

With one of the most destructive and wasteful national policies imaginable, we are deliberately keeping almost a million men and women out of the labor force and denying them the skills they will need when they are released from prison to reenter the labor force. And if this isn't enough, for every would-be breadwinner incarcerated, we can probably add a family to the welfare rolls.

To change the system, like changing welfare, means bucking a powerful prison industrial complex. Huge vested interests—both business and labor—vehemently oppose change.

But how long can a nation, even one as rich as America, continue to support a permanent underclass of 5 to 6 million people who are being paid not to work?

Oh, yes, and there's the 6 million government bureaucrats who are being paid—handsomely we might add—to keep these folks from working.

To continue such policies a nation would have to be not only rich, but stupid.

———

As we look around us, again we ask, "Is there hope?"

Yes. But there is no one answer, no simple solution, for recapturing the work ethic in American life. It is a task that must be approached on many levels.

The problems in our cities, our schools, and our businesses are not going to be cured by technological, psychological, or governmental solutions, important though some of these are. The death of the work ethic in America is a direct result of the loss of a spiritual center in our society. In aggressively seeking to expunge religious values from all of public life, the leaders of the revolution also tore the moral heart out of that life.

Since our view of work flows out of our view of life, we must change the underlying values by which people choose to live. In other words, we must reawaken the conscience of our culture. To do that, we must penetrate what the great English statesman and father of modern conservatism, Edmund Burke, called the "moral imagination." This consists of the whole array of social and moral assumptions widely shared by a people—what earlier cultures called tribal myths or the folklore of society. Our attitudes toward diligence, work, and excellence are part of this cultural consensus or moral imagination.

So the first task is one of moral education at every level—in the home, in the church, in the schools, in the universities, in the corporate world, in media, in government, and among the cultural elite who influence our national priorities and agenda.

Then, because education is so vital in providing motivation and training and skills for young people, the educational establishment has to be radically overhauled. Competition and accountability have to be brought back to America's schools.

And a major reform—a better word might be a counterrevolution—is necessary in government policy to liberate the millions we have imprisoned in the warm embrace of paternalistic government aid programs. We need to free our subsidized, permanently dependent underclass, and since many of the men of that underclass are in prisons, we must take meaningful work into the prisons.

Finally, American business and labor must fundamentally reevaluate the rules of the marketplace. We—all of us—have to change the way we treat and care about work and workers.

Where to begin? As is the case with most problems, with the individual.

PART 4

Restoring the Work Ethic

I cannot believe that this country cannot come together around some values . . . what these kids need is a moral life . . . the issue is not ideas, it's conduct. . . . The real question is how we reach these young people morally, and what do we bring to them.

Robert Coles[1]

8

Transforming the Culture

"I'm doin' this for y'all," he'd say, "so y'all don't have to work for the white man, so y'all don't have to take what I had to take." Then he'd say things like "there's no problem that elbow grease can't solve," or "Old Man Can't is dead. I helped bury him." That sort of upbringing clearly affects your sense of justice, technique—everything—not only intellectually, but emotionally.

Judge Clarence Thomas[2]

Now, LET'S WELCOME OUR NEWEST American hero!" the moderator proclaimed as the tall black man walked vigorously to the podium of the Allen Temple Baptist Church. Enthusiastic applause and whistles continued unabated as the speaker laid a notebook before him and adjusted his glasses, obviously moved by the praise and award he'd just been given at this Fourth Annual Conference on the Black Male.

Beyond the lights and cameras of the media, a standing-room-only crowd filled the borrowed hall. Some were members of the community and the church, but most were kids from local high schools.

Dressed in the running suits and athletic shoes they usually wore to school, they filled the pews and overflowed into the chairs set up in the aisles. In the balcony a few young men lounged with their feet on the railing and their arms around their girl-friends.

Potential troublemakers, the speaker thought. He had some reason to be worried. Most of the young people in the room came from high schools where gangs roamed the halls, where stabbings were a weekly occurrence, and where drugs were done openly. More than half the young women in these schools became pregnant before their junior year.

Sprawled across the second and third rows down front sat a group of adolescents from nearby Loscerros Detention Center who had been furloughed to hear him speak, their lanky bodies encased in acid-washed jeans and T-shirts.

The mid-morning sun shone through stained-glass windows depicting a brown-skinned Christ with flared nostrils; on the opposite wall great figures of African American history glowed with the transfused light.

As he arranged his notes on the podium, the speaker wondered how his message would be received. No doubt they were expecting him to blame the problems in their schools and communities on The Man and his white institutions. That's all they'd ever heard, but they wouldn't hear it from him.

"I come here today not only in my official capacity, but as a black man and father of three," he began, leaning across the podium. "And I know the score." His eyes slowly swept the room as he focused in on the young men gathered before him.

"You are an endangered species living in a culture of violence—and you are the only ones who can do anything about it. Oh, sure, the government has a role to play in stopping violence and drugs and AIDS and all that. But what is far more important is what we are doing to help ourselves and what we are doing to help each other."

"You want to make something out of yourselves," the speaker continued, "it is up to you. You can start by getting rid of drugs. Clean it up, friends. And that means not just speed and crack; it means alcohol too. You guys think it's cool to get boozed up? Not cool. Stupid."

Snickers echoed through the crowd, along with surprised expressions. Kids nudged each other or shrugged their shoulders.

But as the speaker's voice became passionate, the scuffling and whispers subsided and even the guys in the balcony sat up and listened.

"The black community was able to endure two hundred years of slavery and more than eighty years of segregation. Why? Because we maintained that sense of community and connectedness with one another. Even in the wake of slavery, intact families were the norm in the black community, not the exception as they are today. . . . In many respects, we survived better as a people back then. And it is time to remember what worked in our own social structure."

Now murmurs from the audience encouraged the speaker.

"That's right. . . . You tell it!"

"Solutions to the problems of the black community will be found within the black community. We must transform a culture of violence, which defeats and destroys, into a culture of character, which uplifts and empowers. We need strong families—families that spend time together. And families that attend a church, mosque, or synagogue together."

Peering over his glasses and pointing directly at the crowd, he lectured them on finishing school, the need for hard work on the job; he told them to give up drugs, alcohol, even cigarettes. And he talked straight about sex.

"In many of our neighborhoods it is considered a powerful sign of manhood to father a child—or even several children by different women. Don't have sex until you are emotionally ready for marriage and financially ready to provide for your children."

The speaker could read the thoughts on their faces: *Where does he get off? Doesn't he know the score? Who does this dude think he is?*

Well, this dude in the starched white shirt and conservative dark suit was not, as one might have expected, some Bible-pounding preacher or moralizing crusader; he was a medical doctor, former president of Morehouse University, and now a presidential cabinet officer.

Dr. Louis Sullivan, secretary of health and human resources, the man in charge of billions of dollars of welfare aid programs was telling poor inner-city kids that they had to take responsibility for their own behavior.

Three decades of burgeoning social programs have sent one consistent message to the poor: "You are poor because you are deprived and oppressed—victims of the system—and society owes you a way out. And you don't have to do a thing to earn it. Just wait for big paternalistic government to bring the money by the truckfuls."

After thirty years of this paternalism, Louis Sullivan's message was radical stuff—especially coming from a man who is himself a product of this poverty-level, inner-city environment. But Sullivan is not alone—and this is one of the most hopeful signs of the 1990s. A growing movement of men and women from minority communities are echoing Sullivan's message.

Sharon Pratt Dixon, the new mayor of Washington, D.C., has suggested that schools once again be given the authority for corporal punishment for recalcitrant students. Her proposal has been controversial, to say the least. We've had enough counselors, psychologists, and therapy, says the usually soft-spoken mayor. What these kids need is a good dose of discipline. Her words have set editorialists howling with indignation and outrage.

As if on cue, Virginia's Governor Douglas Wilder, the nation's first black governor, picked up the refrain. "Too many young black males have trouble doing hard, honest work and staying out of jail, but no problem making illegitimate babies." The answer? Hard work and sexual abstinence.[3]

The liberal establishment shakes its collective head in disbelief, but William Raspberry is cheering. A respected columnist and, like Sharon Pratt Dixon, a product of the minority community of a generation ago, when both family and church maintained solid values, Raspberry sums up the problem well: "Rights, even when widely distributed and fairly enforced, have not solved our problems. . . . Unfortunately we have spent more time teaching our children about the world's unfairness than about its general tendency to reward effort."[4]

As we go to press with this book, President George Bush has nominated Clarence Thomas to fill Justice Thurgood Marshall's Supreme Court seat. In all of the furor and confusion surrounding the nomination of a conservative black man to the court, Judge Thomas's character has emerged graphically. Thomas was raised by an illiterate grandfather who was humiliated by whites in his hometown of Savannah, Georgia, but who believed in the work ethic.

Thomas was taught that the way to defeat discrimination was through hard work and education. The nuns at his school, he says, "made me pray when I didn't want to and didn't know why I should . . . made me work when I saw no reason to . . . made me believe in the equality of races when our country paid lip service to equality and our church tolerated inequality . . . made me accept responsibility for my own life when I looked for excuses."[5]

What these leaders recognize—and have the courage to say— is that the problems of the inner cities are less structural and institutional than they are behavioral.

The same can be said of the rest of our society. The issue is not what people have, but how people choose to live and what standards they live by. Alexis de Tocqueville called these standards and choices "the habits of the heart" that, when collectively exercised, shape the character and nature of a people.

What we need desperately is a return to the ideal of work as a "habit of the heart."

That means we need to restore America's families. As Secretary Sullivan is fond of saying, the first department of education is the family.

We were fortunate, especially by today's standards.

Jack's father was already in his early forties when Jack was born. His father owned four stores, and his business demands often kept him away from home. When he was home, however, Jack remembers him as a good father. He was firm but fair, and although the family was fairly prosperous, he refused to spoil Jack by giving him too much allowance.

Although his father never pressured him to enter the family business, Jack loved and admired his father and eventually decided he wanted to work for him. When he did, however, he was warned not to expect any special privileges as the boss's son.

"If you go into this business with me, you're going to work harder than anyone else around here. Because your name is Eckerd you will have to work longer hours, and you won't get paid very much the first few years."

{ Jack said okay, and he soon found that he was working not just for the paycheck, but for the excitement of trying to beat the competition in the fast-moving retail industry. }

Chuck's parents were both children of immigrants and sacrificed to give him opportunities they had missed. His mother would cut corners on the grocery budget just to buy him a toy. His father worked all day and went to law school at night during the lean Depression years, but he still made time to spend Sunday afternoons with his son. Father and son would sit and talk on the back steps of their small frame home in a Boston suburb. It was during these times that Chuck's father instilled two important moral lessons: "Always tell the truth" and "do your best, whatever it is."

Chuck's father was not a deeply religious man, but without knowing it, he often paraphrased Martin Luther: "It doesn't matter what you do, whether it's cleaning toilets or being president of the United States—do it to the best of your ability, take pride in your work, and settle for nothing less than excellence."

Chuck took those words to heart and, in one of life's ironic twists, found out what it was like to do both, first in the White House as special counsel to President Richard Nixon, and then in prison where his first work assignment was cleaning toilets.

Be truthful . . . work hard . . . know the value of a hard-earned dollar . . . strive to do your best . . . all are integral parts of America's work ethic. With hard work there is no limit to what you can achieve, says the American Dream. Our parents instilled that dream in us. But many kids aren't so fortunate.

When both parents work—and admittedly for many it is a necessity—they are forced to leave their young children during the morally formative years from one to six. Sitters or day-care centers can never replace the parents' influence in molding the moral values of their children. When the choice is between the financial flexibility of a two-income family or a tighter budget with one parent at home, the answer should be clear: a well-raised child is worth a whole lot more than a new VCR or microwave.

In fact a tighter budget might even be good for some families. A recent book entitled *Spoiled Rotten—American Children and How to Change Them* argues that when affluent middle-class children are showered with toys and amusements, they lose all sense of value. They are given anything they want and are not taught the value of what they have. "We have middle-class kids who are embarrassed to be seen in K-Mart and it's their middle-class parents who are sacrificing," writes the author. They are, in the literal sense of a good thing gone bad, spoiled rotten. The author's answer—with which we agree—is to teach children there are limits. If they want designer jeans, make them pay for the difference over plain label brands. And let them work for that money. It's part of a value system they'll carry with them for life.[6]

If we're to restore the work ethic, the first step is to teach our children that there is a genuine difference between right and wrong, good and evil, and that there is virtue and value and dignity in work. This must begin when they are toddlers so that it becomes ingrained in their consciousness.

A few years ago two Harvard scholars, criminologist James Wilson and psychologist Richard Herrnstein, undertook a ten-year study to determine the causes of crime.

In 1985 they published what became a landmark book, *Crime and Human Nature*, in which they challenged fifty years of conventional wisdom that said crime was the result of race, poverty, and social oppression. They traced genetic strains between parent and child, environment, race, education, poverty—the whole range of influences. Although they determined that intellect and genetics had some effect on behavior, the primary cause of crime was simply *individual choice*. Those choices, Wilson and Herrnstein argued, were determined by one's moral conscience which is shaped early in life and most crucially by the family.[7]

It is in the circle of the home where children first learn the importance of individual responsibility. Until we reclaim our families and our children, we will never deal with the moral crisis in our society, and we will never restore the work ethic.

9

To the Heart:
A Moral Education

The crumbling . . . of [New York City] is stirring complaints . . . and longings for a man on horseback, some
savior riding to the rescue, wielding power like a sword.
New York, like many other cities, needs a man on horseback, but not that sort. It needs John Wesley.

George F. Will[1]

APART FROM THE FAMILY, NO INSTITUTION can play a more vital and
basic role in moral education and in restoring the work ethic than
the church. All those characteristics we associate with the work
ethic—dedication, excellence, thrift, pride in what we do, industry,
and an ennobling view of work—find their deepest roots in Scrip-
ture and through the centuries have been defined and articulated by
the church.

The post-Reformation church believed that one of its primary
tasks was to help new converts discover vocation; that is, to understand how the individual was to use his or her gifts to serve God in

93

the world. Industriousness, seen in that light, was an act of obedience. "Make all you can, save all you can, and give away all you can," was John Wesley's oft-quoted credo.

Today the call to recover the traditional virtues of the work ethic should ring forth from our pulpits, but the church, along with the culture at large, needs to be re-educated in those virtues.

How often have you heard a sermon on the work ethic or on productivity? Or for that matter on the virtues of hard work, thrift, and respect for property? Why aren't churches teaching vocation as the integral part of life that it is?

One of those who saw this failure of the church earlier in this century was Dorothy Sayers: "In nothing has the church so lost her hold on reality as in her failure to understand and respect the secular vocation." How would anyone remain interested in a religion "which seems to have no concern with nine tenths of his life," she wondered.[2]

For example, the church would tell a carpenter to stop getting drunk and to come to church on Sunday. Fine, but what the church should be telling him as well, Sayers argued, was that "the very first demand that his religion makes on him is that he should make good tables." What use was his piety in church attendance if he was "insulting God with bad carpentry"?[3]

When the church *has* spoken on economic issues, it has usually missed the central message and focused on political matters. That's certainly been true of those on the religious left who have equated Christianity with social justice and even socialism, buying into the utopian myth that social structures are the problem and that social salvation comes through the state.

At least one prominent Christian of this persuasion has recognized this error. John Alexander, former editor of *The Other Side*, a mainstay of the religious left, recently wrote: "It is time those of us with sensitive consciences showed our bleeding hearts by wondering aloud why fewer go hungry in South Korea or Singapore than in Burma and Tanzania. . . . It is also time we admitted that when it comes to producing material goods then the [free] market does quite a job. . . . It's ability to do that is strewn across the face of North America, Western Europe, and Japan. . . . Its productivity cannot be questioned."[4]

But those on the conservative side have been equally at fault by remaining woefully uninformed about issues that they have often regarded as secular or worldly, believing that it is the duty of the Christian simply to win souls for Christ. Or they have equated anticommunism, flag waving, and a general faith in free enterprise with Christianity—a dangerous oversimplification.

Even more destructive are those conservatives who have indulged in a false gospel of materialism packaged in spiritual language. This is every bit as bogus as any social utopian program and even more deceitful. It is also a complete repudiation of the work ethic. One propagator of this gospel, Robert Tilton, proclaims: "Anything can be named, claimed, or even demanded, whether it is good weather, a new car or financial success, the recovery of lost property."[5]

There is only one word for this: heresy.

What can the church do?

First, the church must reclaim its own heritage. That means preaching and teaching the work ethic. Drill it into youth classes and proclaim it from the pulpit. Teach diligence, excellence, thrift, respect for property, and that through work we participate in Christ's work of redeeming the earth.[6] That is a bedrock theological truth.

Second, the church must teach vocation. Every Christian needs to discover and understand that the individual's calling is at the very heart of faith and that it is imperative that each Christian glorify God with his or her work.

Our work cannot be separated from our witness, argues Carl Henry, one of our most respected contemporary theologians. The work of the Christian "ought not to be of such questionable caliber that it disgraces God, discredits one's employer, and affronts society."[7]

And the church needs to once again proclaim a high view of work through which, as Pope John Paul II puts it, man learns much, he cultivates his resources, he goes outside of himself and beyond himself.[8]

Third, the church must teach ethics.

The Old Testament still offers the best literature on business ethics. The Books of Amos and Isaiah are all about the ethics of work, wealth, and poverty. Biblical truths about honest scales, helping the poor, not cheating others, and paying fair wages are unchanging and profoundly life-changing.

We know of many businessmen who have read these books, and their business practices have been affected. One is Chuck's close friend Tom Phillips who, as chief executive of Raytheon, established an office of ethics reporting immediately to him which promulgated clear ethical guidelines and invited all employees to seek ethical counsel.

Fourth, whenever and wherever it has preached a false health-and-wealth gospel, the church needs to repent. The church must proclaim a message that convicts individuals of their own responsibility. "If a man will not work, let him not eat" were not compassionless words; they were a call to individual responsibility.

"Man's physical life is dependent upon production for human survival," reminds R. C. Sproul. "Unless we produce food, we will starve. Unless we manufacture clothes, we'll be naked. Unless homes are built, we'll be shelterless. God does care about the human body as well as the human soul, and so production becomes a vital ethical concern for Christians."[9]

In short, the church must teach biblical truth. The church is always worrying about being relevant. It would be difficult to imagine a more timely and relevant message to give the world today.

But the church is not the only institution capable of recognizing the moral vacuum in our society. Believe it or not, in media, academia, politics, and the arts there are encouraging stirrings of a longing to reawaken America's soul.

In 1980 the Moral Majority began flexing its political muscle. Led by Jerry Falwell, this organization of the religious right promised a return to traditional American values. But the media of the day painted Falwell and his compatriots as fundamentalist extremists and Bible-pounding bigots, and most of their agenda failed. A decade later Falwell was back on his Liberty University campus, the Moral Majority disbanded.

Today, Falwell and his cohorts have been replaced by some of the very people who opposed them most vigorously. Television producer Norman Lear, who formed People for the American Way specifically to oppose the Moral Majority, says now, "I look at the '90s and this country suffers a deep spiritual malaise, and nobody is appealing to it."[10] Lear faults both the religious right and the mainline churches for failing to do so. (For anyone confused by this—as anyone who can read must be—that's the same religious right that he did everything in his power to destroy ten years ago.)

Lear seems to be joining Governor Wilder, Mayor Sharon Pratt Dixon, William Raspberry, and a growing number of concerned citizens who are advocating a return to traditional values.

Then there's "Nightline's" Ted Koppel who sounded like an Old Testament prophet when he told a Duke University graduating class: "What Moses brought down from Mount Sinai were not the Ten Suggestions. They are commandments."

An equally strong comment came from columnist George Will, who with customary eloquence suggested that what America needs is a John Wesley, who "rode Britain's rural roads and city streets, evangelized the underclass, exhorting pride and combating family disintegration by reforming behavior."[11]

Basic moral concepts such as right and wrong, long derided by the gurus of the therapeutic professions, are mounting a comeback. Even eminent psychologists are urging a return to the basics. One of these, Garth Wood, shelves psychological nostrums for what he calls "moral therapy."[12]

Wood believes that life is not about the selfish search for pleasure but the contentedness and self-respect that come from duty, love, sacrifice, and the facing of—not avoiding—life's hardships.

"We are happier," says Wood, "when we follow our conscience, not when we deny it. Evil exists and cannot be explained away as neurosis or illness. Friends, family and ministers of religion play an important role in moral therapy. And unlike expensive psychiatric treatments and the 'mind candy' of tranquilizers, moral therapy is free."[13]

Even some of our most esteemed educators are acknowledging that moral reform is vital. Cities, schools, corporations, and government agencies must be revitalized if America is to regain its competitive role in the world, says Derek Bok, president of Harvard, a bastion of relativism. But there can be no such revitalization without a moral renewal that will restore a sense of personal responsibility among individuals. Bok even uses the term *moral education* to describe the task of the secular university. Noble sentiments reminiscent of an age before the revolution—but a sign of hope, nonetheless.[14]

Another keen social observer, an unfailing prophet of social trends over the past three decades, forecasts a return of traditional morality. It was Tom Wolfe who accurately dubbed the 1970s the "me" decade, and, as we mentioned earlier, his novel *Bonfire of the Vanities* captured the spirit of the 1980s. Now Wolfe predicts that the nation is entering an era of "moral fever," in which the 1980s' obsession with affluence will be replaced with a search for religious values.[15]

Business people are discovering that where moral values are preserved, where there is a healthy moral consensus, the work ethic thrives. Evidence of this was seen in a recent "Good Morning America" feature that cited Salt Lake City as one of the most attractive business locations in the country. According to the business people interviewed, this can be attributed to the abundant supply of well-motivated young workers and the low incidence of drugs and alcohol.[16]

Could it be that America's cultural elites are finally under-standing the consequences of the cultural revolution of the 1960s? That a free society, as our founders argued, depends upon a healthy moral consensus? We certainly hope so. Because for good or ill, these cultural leaders will play a leading role in developing that consensus.

10

Back to Basics

If an unfriendly foreign power had attempted to impose on America the mediocre educational performance that exists today, we might well have viewed it as an act of war. As it stands, we have allowed this to happen to ourselves. . . . We have, in effect, been committing an act of unthinking, unilateral educational disarmament. . . . Part of what is at risk is the promise first made on this continent: All regardless of race or class or economic status, are entitled to a fair chance and to the tools for developing their individual powers of mind and spirit to the utmost. This promise means that all children by virtue of their own efforts, competently guided, can hope to attain the mature and informed judgment needed to secure gainful employment and to manage their own lives, thereby serving not only their own interests but also the progress of society itself.

A Nation at Risk[1]

POLLY WILLIAMS IS A ROUND-FACED woman whose genial smile, framed by gray, curly hair, could make her anyone's favorite aunt.

But there is steel in her eyes, the steel that brought her out of the ghetto and into the halls of power.

As a single parent and welfare mother, Polly Williams raised four children and then graduated from college herself. A lifelong Democratic activist and former member of the radical Black Panthers, she gained statewide prominence as the manager of Jesse Jackson's campaigns in her home state.

In her inner-city Milwaukee neighborhood and through her own children Williams saw firsthand the total failure of the school system. Convinced that the educational bureaucracy would never reform itself, when she was elected to the state legislature, she introduced one of the first education choice bills in the country. Her proposal, although limited in scope and largely experimental, was radical. Williams proposed giving vouchers to a thousand low-income Milwaukee students worth $2,500 for tuition in any school they chose—less than half the cost of educating a child in the public system. The public schools could not complain because they would lose no money; nonetheless the counterattack came fast and furious.

One Milwaukee alderman acknowledged that the public school system was "not perfect," but it was "the only one that pretends to educate all the children."

Williams agreed that "pretends" was the right word. "If you keep giving money to the same doctor and the patient stays sick," she replied, "you've got a right to a second opinion."[2]

Williams waged a remarkable campaign, enlisting both conservatives and liberals, and the bill passed the Wisconsin legislature in 1990 and was signed by Republican Governor Tommy Thompson.

Even after the bill was passed, state educational bureaucrats threw up every possible obstacle by mandating impossible schedules and prohibitive amounts of paperwork. School Superintendent Herbert Grover publicly encouraged the teachers' unions to challenge it as unconstitutional, which they did.[3]

But Williams will not be deterred. She has intensified her campaign, gathering national support. If the educational officials "are worried about their jobs," she says, "they should try doing them better."

After all the comparisons between American students and students from other countries, a report by the National Assessment of Educational Progress came to a very simple conclusion: the superior records of foreign students come "because they work harder."[4] No mysteries. No shortcuts. No education-made-easy primers for students or faculty. Just work. Knowledge is not acquired by osmosis, but by discipline and hard work.

But work to what end? Everybody needs a goal. Yet the educational establishment has aggressively advocated giving up standards and tests as artifacts of a more repressive generation.

A mechanic who can't repair engines or a carpenter who can't drive a nail will soon be looking for another job. Shouldn't the same thing be true in education?

Schools that graduate illiterate teenagers should be shut down, and educators who can't pass basic competency tests should be fired. Unfortunately, education policy and powerful unions make such accountability nearly impossible. Teachers are tenured early in their careers and are often guaranteed regular raises regardless of performance. With guaranteed jobs and salaries, where is the incentive to perform?

National testing has been proposed as one way of imposing accountability on educators. But the National Education Association (NEA), a well-funded lobby, has thwarted all attempts to mandate such testing. After all, who wants to be forced to earn a paycheck that was previously practically an entitlement?

Changing our schools must begin with changing the men and women who teach in them. Unless they are held to a high standard of excellence, we will never solve our national apathy.

That same work ethic and that standard of excellence need to be applied to students. If young people don't see the tangible results of their work, or lack of work, in the form of grades and awards, they will be completely unprepared if we begin demanding excellence in the workplace.

Well, you may be saying, we aren't going to change the educational colossus; we've tried. And you're right. The present educational monopoly seems impervious to change.

John E. Chubb, a senior fellow at the Brookings Institute, the nation's premier and historically liberal think tank, along with Terry Moe, formerly of Brookings and now a professor at Stanford, conducted a ten-year study of twenty thousand students, teachers, and principals in five hundred public and private schools across the country. Their conclusion: "Existing institutions cannot solve the problem because they *are* the problem."[5]

WHAT'S NEEDED: THE FREE MARKET

It's time for a revolution in the classroom, they say, and we agree. Nothing less than a massive overhaul of our educational system will do the job. What it needs is a healthy dose of competition. The only way that is going to happen is if parents are given the power to choose the education they want for their children. In other words, free-market education. This is the kind of thing our friend Dr. Jim Dobson and a few other valiant individuals have been advocating, but politicians have fought it.

Polly Williams understands why politicians resist change. They have both created and exploited a dependent class that serves as the base of their political power. "Our liberal friends have built their whole lives around taking care of us," she said, "and they still want to feed us with Pablum. At some point, we want real food. We want to make our own decisions, whether our liberal friends like it or not."[6]

Mike Holt, editor of *Community Journal*, a black Milwaukee newspaper, agrees. To understand the mind-set of these "self-proclaimed liberals," said Holt, "one need only understand that parental choice initiatives would empower African American parents to make educational choices for their children just as white middle class families and Democratic liberals do. It all boils down to empowerment."[7]

Americans across the board agree with Holt and with Polly Williams. According to a Gallup Poll, 64 percent of public school parents favor allowing families to choose which school their children would attend; a full 67 percent of nonwhites said they favored choice.[8]

And no wonder. Competition works. Students in private Catholic schools beat public school students by an average of 4.5 percent in math, 4.8 percent in science, and 12.5 percent in reading. Catholic high school sophomores are four times less likely to drop out than their public school counterparts, and in several areas where comparative studies have been conducted, they are much more likely to go on to college.

American citizens should be outraged by the dismal performance of what one educator calls America's present "totalitarian" educational monopoly. To demand freedom of choice through a voucher system applied across the board is one way competition can be introduced into the educational establishment.

In a voucher system the government would take funds marked for education—our school taxes—and give them to individuals and families in the form of vouchers. The student and his or her family would then be free to patronize the public or private school of their choice. Schools wouldn't get those dollars unless they delivered the goods.

At present, school systems and educators get vast infusions of government money no matter how poorly they perform. A voucher system would give them an incentive to produce by making them accountable to parents who would control the money.

Is this just one more upper-middle-class, conservative attack on public education? Hardly. Those who most eagerly embrace the idea are those who stand to gain the most through an education—inner-city families struggling on the edge of our economy.

President Bush has already broken the political ice. In April 1991 he announced a plan to create incentives for states to adopt choice plans. As Polly Williams found, the backlash from the educational establishment may be intense, but this is a cause worth fighting for.

Standards and Discipline

In order for choice plans to succeed, we need standards and achievement tests so that the performance of schools and teachers can be measured. These will also help restore discipline in education, which is urgently needed at all levels, including higher education, controversial though that is in today's environment.

It has become fashionable at our most prestigious universities to rewrite curriculum requirements to rectify the supposed cultural bias toward Western civilization. At some universities the traditional Western civilization requirements—often a student's only exposure to Plato, Darwin, Shakespeare, and Freud—have been dropped. Instead, students may be required to study "the politics of oppression" or gay and feminist literature. Even basic courses in sciences and math are giving way as the university is gradually turned into a pathway to political empowerment rather than an education fitting graduates for vocation and community life.

What can be done? Government standards won't change the university, but alumni and public pressure can. Take a lead from the Bass brothers of Texas who have given millions to Yale on the condition that the funds be used to teach Western civilization. Or you can refuse to give at all if your favorite university has abandoned the pursuit of truth in favor of some trendy cause.

But not everyone goes to college. Nor should they.

For the majority of high school students, graduation means not freshmen orientation, but finding a job.

Training for the Workplace

Educators should take a cue from economist Thomas Sowell, who refuses to recognize any difference in importance or intelligence between a professor of sociology and a transmission repairman. Luther would applaud. It's the same point he made in the Reformation that so profoundly changed the view of vocation.

One state has taken bold action just this year to upgrade vocational education. Oregon launched a long-range program for restructuring and improving its educational system, called the Oregon Educational Act for the Twenty-First Century. Under the plan, high school students would receive a "certificate of mastery" in the tenth grade and then be steered toward a college preparation program or vocational training. The reforms would also lengthen the school year from 175 days to 220 days by the year 2010.

The critics aren't silent, of course, accusing the state of "adopting an elitist, European-style system in which students not bound for college are pushed into early training for factory work." But the program's chief sponsor says, "It will put the state at the head of the class when it comes to producing students who will be able to keep up with changing technologies in the global economy.[9]

Vocational students deserve respect and a solid education that teaches diligence, productivity, and the dignity of honest labor. To be productive and trainable employees, they need basic reading and math skills; to be discerning citizens they need critical skills; and to be well-informed members of their community they need a general knowledge of history, literature, and political science.

In this area we can again learn from our foreign competitors such as Germany and Japan, who insist that virtually all students reach a high educational standard. "Professionalized" education is provided for non-college-bound students to prepare them for their trades and to ease their school-to-work transition. They operate comprehensive labor market systems that combine training, labor market information, and job search programs comparable to some of our college career placement services.

We need to provide such services for our students. If we don't, we will lose our next generation of workers—the nonprofessional labor force that is the backbone of our economy.

11

Freeing the Slaves

I'm always looking for a better job. . . . Once I get
bored that can make me think of going back to get high,
and I don't want to even think of going back.

Katie Brown, longtime welfare recipient[1]

To put people behind walls and bars and do little or
nothing to change them is to win a battle but lose a war.
It is wrong. It is expensive. It is stupid.

Warren Burger[2]

*The U.S. government has removed 6 million Americans—over 5
percent of the nation's work force—from society and isolated them in
controlled colonies where they are fed, clothed, and housed. Tough laws
are enforced to see that they don't work and to keep them in a state of
vegetative dependency. The qualities of indolence and indifference are
actively cultivated and rewarded. Most will remain in this colony forever. They are citizens of the state, but they have nothing to do.*

IF YOU WERE TO READ SUCH A REPORT in today's newspaper, you
would dismiss it as absurd, or something taken from a futuristic novel.
Yet this is precisely what is happening in America. Government

policies have created a new society, mainly in the inner cities and prisons, of six million citizens with no place to go, nothing to do, doomed to a life of nothingness. And the numbers are increasing each year at a staggering cost.

Why are we stubbornly perpetuating this kind of welfare culture while just about everyone else in the world is rejecting it as counterproductive and inhumane?

Even as we write, the Soviet government, incredible as it may seem, is in the process of renouncing Marxism and attempting to jettison the welfare state in a desperate effort to resurrect their shattered economy. Recent reports from Holland and Sweden, those social welfare pioneers, acknowledge the bankruptcy of the welfare state and how removing incentives has destroyed the work ethic. Because of Holland's generous welfare, one in six workers remains at home drawing benefits for psychological or physical disabilities, twice the ratio as across the border in Germany. "Our welfare state was meant to provide a safety net, but it has turned into a hammock," said one Dutch industrialist.[3]

In his 1991 papal policy statement, the spiritual leader of the world's largest Christian church might well have had Cabrini Green and its counterparts in mind when he charged that welfare saps "human energies" and produces "an inordinate increase in public agencies, which are dominated more by bureaucratic ways than concern for serving their clients."[4]

But ironically the United States, which has given the world democratic capitalism and proven the moral and economic worth of the free market, now harbors the most unyielding welfare subculture. Why?

Well, we received one frank and blunt answer from a prominent black inner-city leader when we asked him why there was such resistance to change the welfare system. Was it because it might hurt so many poor women and children?

"Oh, no," he replied. "There'd be some folks hurt, but most of us would love it. These people want to work, finish their school, get off the dole."

"What's the problem then?" we asked.

"The politicians," he replied, chuckling at what he perceived to be our naiveté. "You understand how all this works, don't you?"

We shook our heads no.

"Come on, man, where have you been?" he said. "The politicians—I mean our own people—have been telling us for years that we can't do anything, that we've been oppressed by you folks, but that they are going to save us."

Now looking deadly earnest, he continued, "So they made us their slaves. They pumped in the green, all that money—and moved their friends into these fat jobs to run things. And all we have to do is vote for them.

"It's the way it works," he said, "don't you understand? We keep them in power, and they pay us to sit on our bottoms.

"We can change," he said, "most of us would love to. Your problem is those dudes in Washington who feed off us."

He is right. For years an entire political establishment has thrived by exploiting the poor, and they've intimidated those who have sought to reform the system by charging them with callousness—or worse, racism.

Just look at the vicious attack on Clarence Thomas, whose very life story is a threat to the reigning political orthodoxy that has, perhaps with the best of intentions, perpetuated the welfare culture in America.

Can it be changed? Yes, if we have the political will to end government policies that are destroying the work ethic in the inner city.

Sadly there has been no real groundswell demanding change, no political constituency fighting against this kind of exploitation. The time has come to change that—and to set the inner-city prisoners free.

The real villain in the welfare system is Aid to Families with Dependent Children (AFDC), the program that accounts for half of all welfare funds spent in the United States. Although the title sounds benign—compassionate in fact—it is actually a trapdoor into welfare dependency. AFDC is paid to unwed mothers as support for their children, and the more children born without a father in the house, the higher the benefits the woman receives. On the other hand, for every dollar a welfare mother earns on her own, her welfare benefits are cut by one dollar. Since AFDC payments are often more than a woman can earn at minimum wage, the incentives to get pregnant early and never look for work are inescapable.

Radical changes are necessary to reform this system.

First, we need incentives to encourage AFDC recipients to work their way out of welfare dependency, rather than growing more and more dependent on it.

Some states are already attempting this. In one state, for example, benefits are reduced if the recipient's child drops out of school. Another state has proposed that payments be limited to just one child, which reduces the incentive to have additional children simply to get more money. Others require job training of welfare mothers. Good first steps.

But David Ellwood, a liberal welfare expert at Harvard recommends a second step: welfare mothers should be cut off entirely after they've been on AFDC for eighteen to thirty-six months. This sounds harsh, but bear in mind, Ellwood is not suggesting that aid to all welfare recipients, such as payment to the disabled who would work but can't; rather he proposes cutting aid to the three to five million hard-core cases who make up more than half of all welfare recipients—the young mothers who get on welfare through AFDC and stay there permanently, as a way of life.

Congress has begun to search for some major welfare reforms. In 1988 it passed the Family Support Act, which attempts to enforce child support. Currently only about half of the women owed child support get what they are due, and a quarter get nothing at all, leaving them largely dependent on AFDC. This statute would require by 1993 that child support be withheld from the absent parent's paychecks, right along with social security and taxes. It also sets uniform child support guidelines and imposes them on courts.[5]

The intent is that absent parents, whether divorced or never married, will be expected to support their children. And since child support is an entitlement from parent to child, it should not create, as welfare has, a disincentive for the custodial parent to work.

Unfortunately, these reforms of the Family Support Act are still only goals. What Congress has mandated will not happen without enabling legislation from individual states—and that will require grassroots political pressure.

No matter what system we adopt to curb government welfare dependency, there will always be some who need help, but in these cases the church and private philanthropy, not government, should be the first place we turn, just as we did a century ago, before the Great Society's not-so-great policies took hold.

In a brilliant article, University of Texas Professor Marvin Olasky chronicles American charity at the turn of the century when charity truly lived up to its name and definition of compassion and benevolent goodwill. Tens of thousands of local charitable agencies and religious groups around the country were intimately involved in the lives of the poor. They visited them in their homes; they taught them basic living skills and helped them find jobs. Many even took abandoned mothers into their own homes, training them to work and integrating them back into family and community.

In Boston alone, Olasky said, "500 people each year took 500 alcoholic or drug-addicted women into their homes—often with their infants—to give them shelter and a place to begin a new life. The poor were not given alms, but the tools to create independence and dignity in their lives. One group over the course of eight years raised 4,500 families out of the rut of pauperism into proud, if modest, independence, without alms."[6]

The charity of one hundred years ago was not one of entitlement, but of ennoblement.

But there is one tragic problem here that distinguishes the poverty culture today from any other time in history.

In 58 percent of inner-city families (which amounts to 24 percent of all American families) there is no father. The "feminization of poverty," as one writer calls it, has had devastating consequences: There is no way to transmit from one generation to the next the traditional role of the male provider for the family, and the problem compounds with each passing generation.[7]

Where are the men?

An overwhelming number of them are in prison, where they, too, are trapped in a culture of enforced indolence.

In 1977 a riot erupted inside the maximum security penitentiary at Thomaston, Maine. It was the right kind of riot.

For years prisoners had been allowed to earn money by using the prison workshop to make lamps, stools, and various novelties, but the amount of money they could earn had always been restricted. In 1977 the warden raised the limit to $10,000, at which point the forces of free enterprise quickly took over. Inmates began whittling, carving, sanding, and gluing wherever there was enough space for a single worker.

"Hey, they were making things all over," said a prison official. "In the cells, in the basement of the kitchen, in the gymnasium. . . . They had little shops all over the place. They were working like beavers. We seldom had any problems from the standpoint of fights or other disturbances." The prisoners set up assembly lines and hired other prisoners. Productivity increased to the point where they persuaded the warden to raise the limit to $15,000. They could now help support their families and pay restitution to their victims.

Those who studied the experiment closely concluded that "Offering inmates real pay for real work could motivate them to constructive activity, sustain morale, and drastically reduce traditional problems of discipline."[8]

This surge of enterprise lasted until 1980 when prison officials feared that the power in the prison was shifting to the "inmate entrepreneurs." So they slapped the men in their cells and kept them there for ten weeks. Then they capped potential income and limited work time. Things were never the same again.

No person has more heroically battled for what he labels "factories behind walls" than former Chief Justice Warren Burger. "Do we really want these million people coming out without a skill that they can sell on the outside?" he asks.

Glenn D. Walters and Thomas W. White, members of the psychological staff of the Leavenworth Penitentiary, agree. By discouraging prisoners from working, they say, we have taken "several giant steps backward by providing support to the criminal's general attitude of irresponsibility." [9]

Prison industry is not a new idea. In fact, several successful programs provide outstanding models.

When Fred Braun graduated from Harvard Business School, he established a small manufacturing firm. Eventually he sold his business, made a small fortune, and went looking for some kind of public service he could do. He was soon named to the governor's task force to review Kansas's penitentiary system.

What he saw shocked him. Inmates stretched out on their beds, staring hour after hour at the walls. Their only work was a few hours of picking up trash or cleaning the kitchen. "I began to see why these guys were worse off when they got out than when they went in."

Fred Braun came up with a radical plan.

First of all, he convinced prison officials, legislators, and community groups that the inmates needed productive work, incentives to perform well, and job skills that would prepare them for life outside. Then, backed with his own money, he built a small sheet metal plant near the prison and started manufacturing. Half his work force was inmates and half regular workers. Buses brought the inmates to work every day, where they were paid the same wage as the other workers. A large portion of their wages was returned to the state in the form of room and board and restitution. Best of all, their recidivism rate was about half that of other prisoners.[10]

• In Florida, Jack Eckerd ran the first privately operated prison industry program. PRIDE (Prison Rehabilitative Industries and Diversified Enterprises) is dedicated to operating all of the state's prison industries for job training on state-of-the-art equipment. PRIDE overhauled optical factories, a tire recapping plant, a furniture manufacturing facility, and several garment industries—some forty-seven industries in twenty prisons doing $80 million in volume in 1989. When asked why some other states have not followed Florida, Jack snapped, "Politics!"

During the first seven years of PRIDE's operation, the state received financial benefits of $35 million from profits, capital improvements including new prison industries, and cost avoidance in vocational training. But despite its success and because of special interest pressure, PRIDE's employment has been limited to about 6 percent of the prison population.[11]

• Control Data, a major electronics firm, tested and trained 150 Minnesota prisoners to assemble computers. Inmates did the job one and a half times as rapidly as regular employees, and during one three-month period the error rate of the prison workers was lower than that at any of the company's other assembly units.[12]

• Best Western, the motel chain, established a telephone reservation center in an Arizona women's prison. Since 1981 the company has regularly employed more than 175 inmates. So far 50 have continued with the company after their release, and at least 9 of these have been promoted to supervisory positions.[13]

• In North Carolina, Hugh Morton hired female inmates to handle telephone reservations in the state's Travel and Tourism division. The operation has saved taxpayers substantial amounts and freed up valuable space.

• During Operation Desert Storm, convicted drug traffickers, bank robbers, and Mafia members in the federal prison at Petersburg, Virginia, assembled wiring for jet fighters and desert lighting for Marine Corps forces in the Persian Gulf.[14]

• The Chino Prison in California trains inmates to be deep-sea divers. Some 90 percent of the graduates find jobs in commercial diving, inspecting dams, bridges, underwater pipelines, and oil platforms. Only 8 percent of the Chino graduates return to crime.

• The Federal Bureau of Prisons has established UNICOR, one of the finest prison industry programs in the country, but even this is resisted by private and political interests.

Encouraging as these are, they affect only a tiny percentage of the prison population. We are, in fact, doing shockingly little. The real models are found overseas.

Between us we have been in prisons in more than thirty countries and have seen the same thing in most that we saw in the Soviet Union. As grim as the Soviet prisons were, like many in the Third World, at least the inmates have meaningful work, a sense of purpose, and almost invariably better morale than the desolate, sullen men and women we encounter sitting idle in their cells in American prisons.

For many of these countries, prison industry isn't even an option; it's a necessity. They do not have the luxury of supporting able-bodied men and women at the state's expense. Inmates need to earn an income, not only to support themselves, but to support the prison system.

One of the best models we have seen is Singapore's Changi prison where ten thousand are confined.

The very name "Changi" sends shivers up the spine of any World War II Pacific veteran, for it was the prison where the Japanese tortured and killed thousands of Allied prisoners. Today, however, like everything else in Singapore, Changi is a beehive of activity.

Private companies have set up factories in various parts of the prison, and they are run with astounding efficiency. At one site inmates assemble sophisticated circuit boards; at another they manufacture beautiful rosewood furniture; there is a large bakery, a printing plant, and a massive crafts area.

The prison industries are managed by SCORE, a quasi-government corporation. Through open, competitive bidding, private industries win the right to run shops inside the prisons. SCORE makes approximately $8 million a year, and the businesses make a profit.

Based on their productivity, inmates are paid a percentage of the going wage for comparable work outside. The men work hard because the more they produce, the higher their pay. Some of their earnings are saved, and some are paid to the prison for room and board.

Prison industries are also large and flourishing in Japan, where private entrepreneurs contract for prison labor. Convicts work in industries such as salvage, metalwork, tooling, and carpentry. They also participate in regular industrial work at the shipbuilding docks where they work alongside noninmate labor.[15]

China employs about 80 percent of its prisoners in a variety of pursuits, including a factory that assembles a thousand new Jeeps and five thousand engines each year. At the Shanghai juvenile facility, young artisans produce Oriental carpets, shoes, binoculars, and handbags.[16] Hong Kong runs similar programs, and their recidivism rate for young offenders is remarkably low.

Even in such poverty-stricken countries as the Philippines and Sri Lanka there are jobs for all inmates, even if only in crafts.

PUT INMATES TO WORK

Prison work programs provide benefits all around. Working prisoners are able to make restitution, pay part of the cost of their own confinement, and in many cases help support their families. Work programs take some of the financial burden of crime and prison off the taxpayers' backs and put it where it belongs—on the offenders—saving government funds in both the prisons and welfare budgets. What we are doing today is an unconscionable waste of taxpayers' money.

They also help the inmates regain their self-respect and prepare them to be contributing, working members of society once they are outside the walls. Fran, an Arizona inmate, calls her work for Best Western "a lifesaver . . . because I had a double negative going for me," since she was over fifty years old and an ex-con. Since her release, she has been promoted three times.[17]

Lawrence Day, now thirty-two, entered jail as a teenager and had never worked a day in his life on the outside. In prison he learned to work a printing press. "I've got a marketable skill," he says. "I've got something to look forward to when I get out of here."[18]

Meaningful work also alleviates the stress of confinement. Georgia prison officials found that a work program brought about a "remarkable transformation in the inmates' attitudes, both about themselves and their environment." As a result of work, "self-esteem and self-worth have increased and individual perspectives have been changed. They take pride in what they accomplish."

We believe that work programs—factories behind walls— should be established in every state and federal prison. It is barbaric not to—the infamous chain gangs of the thirties were more humane than forcing inmates to sit day after day staring at concrete walls and go mad.

Restoring work and the work ethic for one million men and woman in prison should be a top priority on every legislative agenda.

But not all jobs have to be behind prison walls. Over half the men and women in prison today have been sentenced for nonviolent offenses; most pose no threat to society. Many, we believe, could be punished outside the prison—at much less cost—through community-based programs such as work release, house arrest, drug treatment, or mandatory community labor. This allows nonviolent offenders to live at home, support their families, and, most importantly of all, to repay their victims either with a portion of their earnings or with their labor. This is punishment that truly rehabilitates and restores.

• Massachusetts has a program called Earn-It. If an offender refuses to pay back his victims, he will be sentenced to weekends in jail. If he continues to refuse, the sentence is increased. Given the choice, 70 percent of all offenders—and 86 percent of juvenile offenders—choose to repay their victims. Local businesses provide jobs for offenders.

• Over half the states now have restitution programs. Most have authority for it but simply haven't funded it.

• Some work programs do not replace other sanctions, but simply provide an opportunity for inmates to make up in a small way for the damage their crimes have done. Through Prison Fellowship, nondangerous inmates are released to renovate ghetto homes or community centers, or to do other meaningful community work. There are more than fifty such projects a year—like Fullerton, California, where inmates renovated the home of an elderly couple whose wheelchair-bound daughter needed a ramp to get up the front stairs. Or Los Angeles where ten inmates turned two sheds and a house into a live-in treatment center for drug-dependent infants. Or Columbia, South Carolina, where a group renovated a child's playground in the inner city.

These kinds of programs could be multiplied a thousandfold, and everyone would benefit. Again, legislatures need to have the courage to put aside the demagogic lock-'em-up-and-throw-away-the-key rhetoric that has so far given us nothing but the highest crime rate in the world and the most expensive prison system. They need to start legislating work and restitution.

Not to do so would be as criminal as the offenses for which men and women today are locked in prison.

WHAT WE MUST DO

Remember our opening story of the prisoners who threw themselves into the electric fence rather than continue to do meaningless labor? People are created to do purposeful work. For inmates, just as for the rest of us, purposeful work—work to provide for the future, work to create something concrete, work to repay a debt, work to learn a trade—is both a psychological and a moral imperative.

If giving inmates productive work makes so much sense, why haven't states rushed to establish factories behind the walls? The answer, like the answer to the welfare scandal, lies with powerful special interests who have blocked reform. Labor, management, and elected officials all share the blame.

In the early 1980s Arizona attempted to employ inmates at a Cudahy Food Company slaughterhouse. The state branch of the meat cutters union went along, but the union's national leadership killed it.[19]

As one union leader said: "If that means prisoners must continue to be idle, ignorant, living off a welfare state behind bars—all the while plotting the next crime—then so be it. That's not a union problem."[20]

Business can be just as shortsighted. The furniture industry hired a high-powered Washington law firm to scuttle the federal prison industry program called UNICOR. Along with the Ladies Garment Workers Union, they persuaded Congressman Barney Frank to introduce a bill limiting what UNICOR could produce. It passed the House as part of a crime bill. Only when Warren Burger, Jack Eckerd, and others found out about it and phoned key senators was UNICOR saved. But special interests will continue their pressure to maintain our prisons as, in William Buckley's phrase, "the last bastion of socialism in the U.S."

Because of this, most states retain laws that prevent or limit the sale of goods made in prisons. But if we were to adopt a plan whereby businesses compete for the right to set up a factory within the prisons and where wages are set to match productivity, much of the opposition might be lessened.

There are, in fact, some glimmers of hope.

One is the Drug and Crime Emergency Act, sponsored by Senator Phil Gramm and Congressman Newton Gingrich, which proposes repeal of restrictions on the sale of prison-made goods and mandates that prisoners work while incarcerated.

Another is what happened in California when the public was given a chance to vote. For years, former Governor George Deukmejian had tried to get an inmate-labor bill through the legislature, but it was regularly beaten by organized labor. Then in November 1990 the governor succeeded in getting the issue to a public referendum.

It passed, ending the state's 111-year-old ban on the use of inmate labor and enabling the state to contract with private businesses to employ prison inmates. The law mandates wages for inmates that are "comparable" to other workers in the same industry and allows the prisoners to keep at least 20 percent of their wages. The rest goes toward restitution to crime victims and confinement costs.

Although this law is presently stalled in appeals by special interest groups, it is evidence that if the people are given the choice, reforms will come about.

Is this possible? Of course it is. If we care enough.

We cannot afford not to care much longer.

12

Restoring the Marketplace

Work . . . presents moral issues. But we have not attended to them. [We] ignore the other moral considerations having to do with work. We allow people to work only for money. We offer only endless tasks for those who would try to escape confrontation with life, and we encourage their being distracted or pacified through the consumption of goods and services.

Perry Pascarella[1]

No matter how many structures we fix, no matter how many laws we reform, restoring the work ethic in our society ultimately boils down to one thing: We must restore it in the hearts and minds of individuals. It is through the individual—the factory worker, the field foreman, the CEO, the secretary, the volunteer, the fast food server—that the work ethic becomes a reality on the floor of the shop, at the desk in the office, in the boardroom, and on the assembly line.

We've said from the beginning that people simply aren't working as hard as they used to, and we've discussed the historical, cultural, and personal reasons for that. Then we've looked at some proposals that may well revive the work ethic in our homes, schools, churches, prisons, welfare, and other institutions. Now it is time to ask how we can revive the work ethic in the workplace, in everyday life.

As we prepared to write this book we asked ourselves where we saw exciting, successful, and ethically run organizations on the American scene and what these businesses are doing that is different. In each one we profiled, we found a constant: executives, directors, and management had sat down together and developed a clear idea of just why their organization existed and what its goals and values were. That may seem like simple common sense, but in the rush for the profits that keep enterprises afloat, sometimes the values that truly engage the hearts and minds of the people who make those profits get lost.

Then these leaders went a step further and presented the goals and values to the people who worked for them. In case after case, we discovered, it was that shared vision that drove the employees to take their company to the top.

People want to feel significant. They yearn to see how they fit into the big picture. They are willing to work hard, even sacrificially, when they believe that without them the job may not get done. But when corporate purposes and core values are not clearly defined in terms workers can understand, act on, and be held accountable to, employees usually see their tasks as meaningless. Without clearly stated ideals or standards, they will never know whether their jobs have been performed well or whether they have contributed toward the success of the venture.

This is particularly true within large organizations where separate departments are responsible for the various, distinct aspects of the operation. Absorbed by the mechanics unique to their work area, individuals often begin to regard other departments as obstacles rather than teammates with the same goals, and the result is often a work force of isolated parts simply waiting to draw a paycheck rather than a satisfied, efficient, productive unit.

Healthy human beings want to be connected. They want to belong.

When Cummins Engine was founded in 1919, the company explicitly highlighted individual worth and ingenuity as the core of its values, but over the years these were gradually forgotten. As the company grew, they hired managers from Detroit's large automotive firms instead of developing managers from within. These new supervisors, who were not steeped in Cummins's values, neglected the many talents the line workers had to offer; instead they operated by a management system developed at the height of the Industrial Revolution when the assembly line had been broken down into simple tasks the undereducated, mostly immigrant workers of that day could understand. As a result, by the time James Henderson joined Cummins, the company had had seven strikes within a three-year period.

"Accountants and production managers loved that old management system," says Henderson, now Cummins's president, "because they could easily count bolts and widgets as they came along the line."[2] That became the measure of productivity, and it created an ever-widening chasm between the worker and management. It was time for Cummins to return to the basics.

The first step was to develop a set of core values that employees could use to measure their own performance—and be measured by. The list the Cummins team came up with focused on the people:

- trust, respect, and equity for workers
- a commitment to the worker's full potential
- training as a keystone for attaining organizational excellence
- the worker's participation in decision making

Cummins decided to test their new approach in a model plant in South Carolina, and it worked better than Henderson and his associates dared hope. Quality rose, and so did the workers' sense of commitment. For example, two women began drawing a rose on each engine they assembled. Although the artwork was hidden when the engine was painted, the rose was the women's unique statement of their commitment to quality.

In the model plant jobs were no longer broken down into narrowly defined tasks. This took some getting used to, as Jim Henderson learned the day he called the plant manager's office several times and no one answered. When he finally reached the manager at his home later in the evening, Henderson learned that the manager, his secretary, the receptionist, and every other available person in the building had been down on the assembly line all day filling a rush order.

Which values to elevate and the basis for them is sometimes the toughest question for business leaders to answer. Some, like Cummins, turn to their roots; others, like the Aluminum Company of America (Alcoa), turn the spotlight on themselves to redefine purpose and meaning, inviting dialogue between management and workers.

Fred Fetterolf, Alcoa's president, knows every side of the aluminium industry, having worked his way up through the ranks of Alcoa over many years. "I've worked for Alcoa all my life," said Fetterolf, "but we had really never articulated a vision for the company or a set of values that we wore on our foreheads and could be judged by."[3]

Led by Fetterolf and Paul O'Neill, Alcoa's chairman who had distinguished himself as assistant budget director for the federal government, the company spent millions of dollars and thousands of work hours to define and instill six core values into its sixty thousand workers, managers, and executives:

- integrity
- safety and health
- quality of work
- treatment of people
- accountability
- profitability

Once the values were set, O'Neill and Fetterolf faced the task of convincing the workers they were sincere.

Since such moral principles as truthfulness, compassion, and accountability formed the cornerstone of the six values, O'Neill and Fetterolf began talking openly about their own strong personal beliefs, which provided the resolve it took to see new values put to work in the company.

"I used to duck the Christian issue by talking generally about faith and ethics," said Fetterolf. "Now with our new set of values, I felt compelled to get up-front about my Christian convictions. Everyone may not agree, but I believe there is respect for those who declare themselves."

For some time, those new values went against basic, bottom-line business instincts, as Fetterolf discovered when he and a vice president visited one of the company's most remote sites, a bauxite mine in Suriname.

After landing on the single airstrip cut into a lush tropical hillside, the two executives were escorted by the plant manager to the mining site. There they watched an earth mover claw through the rock into the ore. As the operator backed away to position the vehicle for a new approach, two other workers almost stumbled into its path because its safety lights and siren weren't working.

The vice president asked the plant manager why the safety equipment wasn't working and how long it would take to fix it.

"Ordinarily repairs are made at night after the mine shuts down," the manager said. "It could take a couple of hours or more."

"Shut down the mine until that vehicle is repaired," the vice president said firmly.

The news spread fast. Alcoa's management was actually practicing what they preached, placing worker safety above production!

Of course it takes more than one decision to convince workers that a company is serious about new values. Employees wondered if this was just another management whim that would pass when the economy turned sour. They soon learned that the changes were real.

And it has made a difference. The company recently reported that, company-wide, the workdays lost to injuries declined significantly over the last several years.

Jack Reichert, the chairman of the board of Brunswick Corporation, is also a staunch believer in values, and he makes clear in speeches or documents to his employees that his values are based in the Christian convictions he has held for years. Those values include a commitment to "made in America quality," the company's responsibility to its customers, and a concern for "all people . . . their personal dignity and their rights to quality."[4]

ServiceMaster is another company that boldly proclaims its values, which define both methods and motives. The company values are listed prominently in every annual report, displayed in their offices, and talked about at every opportunity:

- to honor God in all we do
- to help people develop
- to pursue excellence
- to grow profitably

In 1981 Peter Ochs started Fieldstone, a Southern California real estate development company, aimed at first- and second-time home buyers, a hard-pressed group during those sluggish economic times. During his first year in business Ochs built and sold eighty-two homes; he now builds close to fourteen hundred homes a year, and his company's revenues have shot to $350 million.

Influenced by Tom Peters's *In Search of Excellence*, Ochs established a set of values to drive his company. Beginning with "the basic Christian belief that God values people," Ochs concluded that "I should value people."[5]

"We actually have a list of values printed on a little card carried by all of our employees." The card lists the following values:

- excellence in everything we do
- an environment of teamwork and trust
- value of the individual employee
- commitment to our home buyers
- executing details well
- integrity in the conduct of our business

"Every family, every college, every corporation, every institution needs tribal storytellers," writes Max DePree, retired CEO and current chairman of the board of Herman Miller, Inc., in his book *Leadership Is an Art*. "The penalty for failing to listen is to lose one's history, one's historical context, one's binding values."[6]

Without a folklore—a stock of core values—which is passed along formally and informally among people and generations, he says, "any group of people will begin to forget who they are."[7]

In a time when individual productivity is at an all-time low and there is a growing mistrust between management and workers, we can't afford to lose that folklore. It is adherence to a set of values that gives focus to our lives, and it is adherence to a set of values that drives us to perform. The question is, what values?

Based on Jack's interviews with these leaders and many others, we have come up with a list of six core values we believe will make a difference in the productivity and morale of any enterprise.

• **The Value of the Worker**   As Luther said, every job is to glorify God, and every worker is infinitely significant. All who labor, no matter how menial their task, must be treated with respect and dignity. That means corporate leaders need to enlist the help of every employee in solving workplace problems. It's the right thing to do—and it's good business.

• **Walking and Talking in the Trenches**   How do you get those values out to the people doing the work? How do you find out what values the worker needs? Ivory-tower management doesn't work; managers need to lead their forces by going to the front lines themselves.

• **Responsibility and the Pursuit of Excellence**   No work that is less than our best can be personally meaningful or rewarding. And no work that is less than our best can be truly profitable. When we encourage excellence, we undercut the corrosive ethic of entitlement.

• **The Value of Training**   Developing the skills of employees is not only good for the individual, increasing loyalty and sense of self-worth; it also makes them more valuable to the organization.

• **Dollars and Sense**   This is the profit motive. We're not so otherworldly as to think that multimillion dollar corporations ought to exist just for the general good, or that people work hard just because they like to. For most, the greatest motivation comes from incentive pay and healthy competition.

• **Working to Serve**   Effective leadership includes enabling others to meet goals. No one said it better than Jesus: He who would lead, let him serve.

We believe that incorporating these six principles into the workplace will not only give workers a sense of the dignity and goodness of work, it will improve productivity and profitability as well. But don't take our word for it. Look at those who have embraced these principles. Their successes speak for themselves.

The Value of the Worker

People are becoming sufficiently displeased, I think. Their lives have had the spirit stripped away. People are looking for new answers, for solutions. They are looking for models.

Tom Chappell, CEO, Tom's of Maine[8]

A SET OF CORPORATELY HELD VALUES and goals is the soul of an organization, and the first of those, the heart of any enterprise, should be the value placed on individual workers.

Jack Eckerd learned this early on. He remembers well the summer of 1959 when he sat nervously outside the office of the president of one of Tampa's largest banks. Jack's weathered briefcase stuffed with the financial reports that proved his young chain of five self-service drugstores was worthy of the bank's support, and he was convinced the figures spoke for themselves. So was George Jenkins, the founder of Publix Supermarkets. Jenkins had just offered Jack the opportunity to open a new Eckerd Drugstore in five new Publix centers around Tampa Bay and also the right of first refusal each time the successful grocer opened one of the hundreds of strip centers springing up throughout Florida. All Jack needed was a bank loan.

But his banker thought differently, as Jack discovered once he got inside the man's office.

"You're trying to grow too fast, Jack," said the bank president. "Take two Publix locations instead of five."

Jack couldn't do that—the deal he'd been offered was double or nothing. He needed funds for five new stores, and he needed them fast. So he scooped up his spreadsheets and calculations, thanked the banker, and headed across the street to talk to the bank's fiercest competitor. Once again he explained his plan as hard as he knew how.

"These numbers and projections are real," Jack said. "I can double my size and profits in two years. The economies of scale will increase each store's purchasing power and decrease its advertising costs."

"Yes, I can see how you could say that," the banker said dryly as he stared out the window overlooking Tampa Bay, avoiding Jack's gaze.

He's going to turn me down, Jack thought. Figuring he had little to lose at this point, he played his last card. Leaning across the bank president's desk, he pointed to the balance sheet.

"You bankers look at my projections, my balance sheet, and my 35 percent annual growth from this new type of drugstore," Jack said insistently. "But you're missing the biggest asset I have. My people. They are the best. You won't find that on any spread sheet, but believe me it's true."

Jack left the bank with a $750,000 loan. His belief in his people had turned the tide.

Over the succeeding years, those employees did indeed help make the difference. And when he was finally in a position to do so, and for the rest of his business career, Jack rewarded his employees' efforts many times over for their part in the success of Eckerd Drugs.

Eckerd's doubled their size and profits on schedule, and large amounts of capital were needed again. Jack's financial advisers convinced him that converting Eckerd Drugs from a privately held to a publicly traded company was the best way to get the capital to continue growing. Within weeks of going public the stock price almost doubled.

"Well, Jack, you're a wealthy man," said his attorney, referring to the proceeds from newly issued shares of Eckerd stock. "Only on paper," Jack quipped. "And besides, it's not all mine."

"What do you mean? It was your company and you only sold a small part of it."

"Yes, but some of the rest belongs to my employees. They deserve to be cut in on the action. They also worked hard to build this company."

"You mean you want to sell them some of the stock at a reduced rate?"

"No," Jack said, "I want to give them some stock! On some sort of equitable basis. Maybe length of time with the company and the degree of individual responsibility."

The lawyer protested. "The IRS will give us problems. They'll want to charge you a gift tax."

"Well, that's your job," Jack said. "Work it out."

The attorney worked it out. Those Eckerd employees who held onto the stock saw their personal fortunes grow right along with the company's.

But his employees were not the only people Jack cared for. The day he took the company public, he made a silent pledge never to make a business decision unless it looked good for his customers, his stockholders, and Eckerd Drug employees.

Eckerd also responded to his customers' needs and concerns, not just their buying power. In 1971 a concerned grandmother wrote complaining about the risque books sold on Eckerd's book racks. She did not like a paperback her fourteen-year-old grandson had purchased at Eckerd's. She sent Jack a copy in which she had underlined the steamy and provocative passages. Jack was shocked. Within forty-eight hours the books came off the shelves, along with *Playboy* and *Hustler* magazines.

"Mr. Eckerd, we'll lose $3 million in sales by eliminating those books from the racks," his vice president told him.

"I don't think we'll lose anything," Jack replied, "because our customers trust us to do the right thing. After all, we *do* advertise as

'America's Family Drug Stores.'"

Sales the next year increased 43 percent.

Valuing people means investing in them just as you would invest in capital equipment. And just as machinery needs oil, people need to see a tangible return for their work and need to know that they are valued not just for a single task—or for the money they spend—but for the variety of skills and insights they might have.

Sometimes that means giving workers the freedom to fail.

Terry Hershberger, chairman of Indiana-based Security Group, Inc., is a self-deprecating man who enjoys his rough-edged image. He and a partner bought out Security Group when it was failing, trimmed the payroll, increased profitability, and soon had the company turned around, using some rather unorthodox down-home methods. He not only encouraged employees to make decisions and take responsibility for their own work, but he also removed the fear of failure, the fear of suddenly losing a job that a former heavy-handed management had used, in his words, "to beat up on them."

"I'd go around putting twenty dollar bills in people's hands when they made a mistake," Hershberger explained. "I would say 'Congratulations! I understand you made a big flop. Here's twenty bucks—go fix it.' They didn't know what to think. But it sure did get their attention."[9] By giving his employees the freedom to fail, he let them know that they weren't going to be fired for a momentary lapse, that they were more valuable to him than any individual piece of work they did.

There's nothing more important to a worker than that sense of importance. When people feel that their efforts are not valued, it can create a real labor crisis—as it did at a Pennsylvania steel company named Pittron.

Wayne Alderson, the tall, lanky son of a coal miner, served as a scout on the Siegfried Line during World War II. His greatest battles, however, were fought back home on the job in the tough Pennsylvania steel mills.

On October 26, 1972, steel workers struck the Pittron Company where Alderson was chief financial officer. The workers complained that management had reneged on a promise to pay back benefits from a previous year, but other issues simmered as well. Matters of dignity and personal respect and working conditions were very real, and very hard to bring to the bargaining table.

Although he was part of management, Alderson didn't believe in the confrontation and intimidation that Pittron management was known for. He sympathized with the workers' plight. It was time for a change.

Alderson began walking the floor of the plant with the employees, learning their names and listening to their problems. Slowly he developed his now well-known "value of the person" approach: "If people were valued, prized more than machines or short-term profits, perhaps the other logistical and mechanical problems of management would begin to take care of themselves."[10]

Alderson, influenced by his Christian convictions, stressed love, dignity, and respect. Instead of criticism, he looked for opportunities to pay compliments. He took a personal interest in the men on the foundry floor and got to know them well.

His "Operation Turnaround" worked—in spite of opposition from hard liners in both labor and management. Within twenty-one months, sales went up 400 percent, profits rose to 30 percent, employment was up 300 percent, and productivity rose. Grievances and chronic absenteeism practically disappeared. In less than two years, Pittron moved from a deficit of $6 million to a profit of $6 million.

Alderson's emphasis on the dignity of the individual changed the workers' attitudes and improved their performance.

"My work changed," said foundry worker Jim Mordecki. "I put more of myself into it. I started to do my job with special care. I took pride in what I was doing."[11]

Joseph Odorcich, a steel worker and local union official, said that before the turnaround "I was just another number" in a filthy plant. But "somebody recognized that these [workers] are people. Treat the people decently and the work you will get out of them will be much more than if you high-pressure them."[12]

Pittron's profitability made it an attractive commodity in the sagging steel industry, and eventually it was sold to another company that looked hungrily at the bottom line of Pittron's balance sheet but failed to see its greatest asset: its motivated workers.

"Operation Turnaround" succumbed to "Management Turn Down" as, one by one, Alderson's "value of the person" programs were dismantled. A few months after the purchase Alderson was forced out. Seven years later, Pittron shut down. Management cited economic reasons as the cause, but Alderson asserts that "if the truth be told, Pittron's return to a dog-eat-dog management style reduced the company to a shambles."[13]

Frank Brock, of the Brock Candy Company and now president of Covenant College in Lookout Mountain, Georgia, provides a compassionate and concrete example of how respect for individual workers helped him turn his business around.

Frank Brock has always had the loose gait and "gee wiz" manner of a boy from Tennessee; at twenty-nine years of age, he looked nineteen. Straight out of a hitch with the Air Force and with his Harvard Business School diploma in hand, he felt less than confident about taking over the family business. He had the right last name to become the executive vice president of the Brock Candy Company, but little else. Still, he was determined to run the business. It was in his blood.

Initially Frank spent 90 percent of his time at the plant just learning the ropes. Often he felt that he was on the ropes himself. Brock's market share was plummeting, and he had to find out why.

It was then that the young executive remembered the advice his Air Force commanding officer had given him: "A general can't fight a battle from the War Room. He's got to get to the troops."[14]

So Frank assembled his troops, the men and women on the line—bakers, candy boilers, and assembly operators.

"You folks know more about candy making than I'll ever know," the soft-spoken Brock told them. "Some of you have been at it longer than I've been alive. So tell me, what's wrong?"

The workers shifted nervously. Sensing their anxiety and the reason for it, Frank reassured them. "People, trust me when I tell you that what you say in this room will stay with me. No manager is going to hassle you because of it."

Evelyn, the chief baker who had been with Brock for almost twenty years, looked up at Frank and sighed heavily. "If you want to know what's wrong with the candy, Mr. Brock, just ask one of my kids. They'll tell you there's more scrap in the bag than there is whole candy."

"That crazy German ordered us to throw some of the crushed candy scraps into every bag to get the weight up," Evelyn reported, referring to Brock's autocratic and immensely unpopular predecessor.

"If you want to know why Brock candy ain't sellin', that's it. Or at least part of it," observed Delmer, a key operator on the assembly line.

"That will be changed. Today!" Frank declared. "Now what else do I need to know?"

Gradually the workers opened up, telling him ways they thought quality and production could be improved. Some were helpful, others were not. But the young manufacturer learned his first important lesson: People want to work, and they want to take pride in the products they produce. And the workers learned something, too: Their boss would listen, and he cared about them as people, not just as cogs in a machine.

After the meeting, Evelyn held back until the others had left. "Mr. Brock, there's something else you may want to know about.

You know Delmer, the operator in assembly?" Frank nodded. "Well, Mr. Brock, he hasn't got any water in his house. Maybe someone could look into it." Then she scurried from the room, afraid she had said too much.

A few days later Frank drove up into the foothills surrounding Chattanooga, around treacherous curves and through cuts in the rugged mountain, to the small town where Delmer lived. There he found that Delmer not only had no running water, but that his wife, Mildred, was bedridden.

Deeply moved by their plight, Frank began to look for some solutions. A water line, he discovered, ran along the main road that led to the rural home. It wouldn't take much to dig a line a quarter of a mile up the hollow to the house. Evelyn agreed to recruit a couple of men from the plant to help, and Frank provided the materials. Before long, Delmer and Mildred had "runnin' water."

At the next meeting of Frank's new Employee Task Force, Evelyn said: "Mr. Brock, we all know what you did for Delmer, and we want you to know that we all appreciate it. We just want to say thanks." Then, following the meeting, she walked right up and addressed her boss confidently: "Mr. Brock, you know we've got no windows in this plant?" The following year the workers at Brock Candy Company moved into their new, sunlit facility.

Frank's eyes still sparkle when he remembers those early days and the wellspring of wisdom he found in his employees. His deeply held belief that each individual is valuable enabled him to lead effectively, make better business decisions, and encourage greater productivity from his employees.

———

It would be unrealistic to suggest that managers can become personally involved in the lives of each worker. But a sense of intimacy and mutual trust can be instilled in the workplace when managers show genuine concern for the individual employees.

Walking and Talking in the Trenches

Leaders don't inflict pain—they share pain.

Max DePree[15]

Wᴡᴇɴ ᴛʜᴇ ᴊᴀᴘᴀɴᴇsᴇ ʙᴇɢᴀɴ ᴛᴏ ʙᴜɪʟᴅ factories here in America, they avoided major urban areas in favor of more rural settings. Union bosses, politicians, and journalists howled, accusing the Japanese of being racist because they were avoiding the inner-city poor and unions.

The charge was false: the Japanese sought the middle-American people because of their farming background, strong family ties, and willingness to learn and perform many different tasks. The Japanese were looking for employees who had something extra to bring to their line jobs—creativity, a broad range of skills, and the ability to look at a problem from several different perspectives.

But it's not just farmers who have the ability to think beyond the five feet of conveyor belt at their station. Most workers, given the chance, will prove to have skills and creativity that remain untapped by autocratic management.[16]

In the early 1980s Jim Henderson of Cummins Engine visited Japan where he saw workers and managers laboring together to improve quality and increase productivity. Henderson returned home determined to adopt the best of what he had seen: a management style built on the belief that line workers can help solve problems.[17]

In Cummins model plant in South Carolina this meant letting the engine assembly workers organize themselves into work groups around a related set of tasks. They wrote their own work procedures and were responsible for the results. Instead of supervisors, these teams had advisers. When they could not solve a problem or needed guidance, the teams could call in technical assistants. Everyone on the team was expected to learn new skills and improve, not because management demanded it, but because the team members expected it of themselves and each other.

There were some surprises.

"Leo, we've got ourselves a little situation out on one of our engine assembly teams," Frank, the plant's chief team adviser drawled into the phone one afternoon. "You better mosey on down here and see for yourself."

When Leo, the plant manager, reached the line he saw Mary Beth and Kaye standing rigidly before a fully assembled engine. Kaye had a determined look in her eye, and Mary Beth walked up to Leo as he approached the work area.

"Leo, we've got ourselves an engine here we want you to look at."

"What's wrong with it?"

"There ain't a thing wrong with it!" Kaye interjected. "And that's the whole point."

"Will someone please explain what's going on here?" It was late and Leo had not reviewed the next day's production orders.

"Ever since we started these assembly teams three weeks ago, these yahoos have been sending us for the parts while they've been doing the assembling," Kaye launched in immediately.

"And which yahoos might that be?" Leo asked.

"Jerry and Cleatus," she said, pointing to the two men standing a few feet away. "Our so-called teammates who live in the dark ages where men do the steppin' and women do the fetchin'."

"We thought that kind of stuff was supposed to end with team work, Leo," snapped Mary Beth.

Leo began to grasp the "situation" Frank had referred to. Apparently the men felt obliged to do the assembly work and "let" the women bring them the parts.

"This is a team, Mary Beth. Jerry and Cleatus were out of line," Leo agreed. "How do you folks want to solve the problem?" He motioned for Jerry and Cleatus to move closer.

"Solve it? They've done it already," Frank howled. "These ladies assembled this engine all by themselves, on their own time."

"We carried our own parts, too," Kaye added with defiance.

"And we tested it," said Mary Beth, her eyes bright with enthusiasm.

"Sounds like you gir—" Leo caught himself just in time, "er, women, have just ended a little run of male chauvinism."

"And built a mighty fine engine," Frank chimed in.

"And taught these two yahoos a little bit about competence, quality, and creativity," Kaye chided her teammates with a smile, quoting from the company's new set of core values.

Several problems were solved that day as the participatory system opened the door to meaningful work, competence, and creativity.

———

We've heard it called everything from "Management by Walking Around" to "Employee Empowerment," but it all boils down to one thing: recognizing that you can learn more in the trenches than you can dream up in the boardroom. This kind of management is built directly on our first principle—the acknowledged value of the individual worker—and begins with a basic belief that people want to work hard, that they want to beat the competition, and that they will level with you. But first you have to ask them.

When you do, it changes workers' whole approach to their jobs. Cynicism and apathy, which presently plague our workplaces, are replaced by a sense of community and ownership of the work at hand.

Take the case of Tom Van Dyk, a farm boy from rural Michigan, who encountered participative management when he began working at Herman Miller in Zeeland, Michigan.

When Tom graduated from high school he had two goals: to marry the girl he'd been dating for years, and to find a job so he could take care of her. Tom had worked on his father's farm all his life, but it provided just enough livelihood for his parents and his older brother's young family. Tom would have to find a good job.

"Herman Miller's a good place to work," a friend told him, "they really care about people there."[18] So following his graduation, Tom put in his application at the company. Less than three weeks later he got a call, then an interview, and was hired for an entry-level job.

During his first few days at Herman Miller, Tom was filled with questions and doubts. After eighteen years on a farm doing a variety of tasks he wondered if he could stand the confinement of factory work and the assembly line. His job—hand-inserting plastic glides into grommets on the bottom of room dividers—was tedious.

One day, not long after he began working at Herman Miller, an elegant and patrician older gentleman stopped by Tom's work station and extended his hand. "Good morning, young man. We haven't met before. You must be a new employee. I'm D. J. DePree."

Tom was thunderstruck. D. J. DePree was the chairman of Herman Miller, the grand old man of the company.

D.J. stayed to chat about Tom's upbringing on the farm, his adjustment to the new job, and ideas for the future.

"We're experimenting with a new panel machine," DePree said before he moved along to another work station. "It could be that with your background with equipment you would enjoy something like that."

Tom learned that the company chairman could often be found out on the line, talking with his employees, and he expected all his managers to do the same—to spend time with employees, listening to them and getting their ideas.

"We call it participative management," another employee told Tom. This co-worker then described Herman Miller's Scanlon system, a program designed to get employee input. "You can suggest anything you think will help, and the company will consider it."

"Consider it and file it in the trash can?" Tom quipped.

"No! Our ideas are taken just as seriously as senior management's. If it can't be implemented, you'll know why not. It's a great system."

After six months Tom was trained on the panel machine, which he then operated for five years. Today, after thirteen years with the company, he is the receiving coordinator unloading trucks of raw material to manufacture the company's line of office furniture. Although he has received regular pay raises, Tom's job-level classification has remained the same, but he isn't complaining.

"There's a feeling of family here that I know I could not get in another job," Tom says. He admits that his own spiritual values were strengthened by watching D. J. DePree, now deceased, and his sons live honestly before the employees. And Tom believes that participatory management has been the key to his success at work.

Participative management is one of Herman Miller's distinctive principles—so distinctive that the name DePree has become synonymous with the principle. Max DePree, who succeeded his father as chairman of the board, describes the concept as central to his company's philosophy of being oriented primarily toward the person and not primarily toward the organization. For workers like Tom this creates a real participation within the workplace where everybody's ideas are listened to and where everyone is invited to be involved.

———————

Jack Eckerd knows the value of getting out of the corporate offices and into the trenches to listen to store employees, cosmeticians, pharmacists, and customers. Discounts for senior citizens and two-for-the-price-of-one photo processing—innovative ideas first introduced by Eckerd's and now common in retailing—came to Jack from chats with employees and customers.

But workers are not the only ones who are encouraged to participate. Customers are a vital, though frequently neglected, source of ideas and feedback—like the customer who complained to Jack about the novels sold in his stores. Many companies rely on cumbersome questionnaires and telephone market surveys that can never replace direct contact with customers.

In 1951 as Jack moved through the aisles of a Sacramento self-service drugstore, he asked himself, "Why do so many innovative retail business concepts begin in California?" Back East customers still had to walk up to the pharmacy counter, ask the clerk for a tube of toothpaste, then wait while the clerk got the correct brand off the shelf, wrapped it up, and rang up the purchase. In California, Jack observed, customers moved around the aisles choosing from an array of products and brands stacked on the shelves or on the floor; they then lined up to check out at the front of the store with shopping baskets brimming.

"Excuse me, ma'am," Jack stopped one woman. "I'm visiting from back East, and I've never seen a store like this before. Do you shop here often?"

"All the time," the customer volunteered.

"This place must be close to your home then."

"Not really. I drive five miles to get here. It saves me time in the long run though. I can get more in this store than I buy in three different stores closer to home. I can choose from so many brands here, and most everything is quite a bit cheaper."

After hearing the same story over and over, Jack returned home and soon launched his successful self-service drug chain. He never forgot what he learned from these simple contacts, or how he learned it. Jack spent nearly 50 percent of his time in the stores—both his and the competitions'—talking to the clerks and customers and looking at the displays.

That's where he learned the lesson of the red rubber balls. One day when he was visiting one of his stores, Jack noticed that a display item—bright red rubber balls—simply weren't selling. Jack started asking why, but no one in management could give him any reason. So Jack went to the clerk. She looked Jack in the eye and stated what should have been obvious: "Children buy rubber balls but these are on the top shelf where the kids can't get their hands on them."

The balls were moved to the bottom shelf and soon sold out.

Inviting input from all levels of the business, including both clients and employees, is essential for nonprofit and charitable organizations as well. "Helping people position themselves where they can make a difference" is the key to success according to Bob Buford, a Texas businessman and philanthropist who founded the Peter F. Drucker Institute for Non-Profit Management.[19]

Some managers are threatened by this participatory system because they see that their traditional views of management and leadership must change. Many managers from the old school believe that any practice that gives employees a significant role in decision making strips managers of some of their power.

They couldn't be more wrong. Management that gets in the trenches empowers all workers, at every level, and the resulting synergy gets things done.

At Fieldstone, Peter Och's home-building firm, participatory management drives decision making down to operational levels.

The employees brainstorm the issues and decide what they want to work on for the year. The questions they deal with range from whether supervisors are communicating with construction managers right down to the nitty-gritty of setting production goals. Creating that environment, says Ochs, "is what it takes to make a company grow."[20] And Fieldstone has grown in spite of the volatile nature of the housing industry.

Ross Perot, who made his fortune as founder of Electronic Data Systems, says spending time with employees is the "number one" priority for a manager. "Number two, any time you have a problem, go straight to the people who are interfacing with the customer and say, 'Okay, what's wrong?' If they trust you, they will tell you since they are out there on the front lines day after day. We don't tolerate anyone looking down on one another. We don't like people to look up with awe either because that stifles communication. We want everybody to look directly at one another."[21]

Even at Alcoa, a heavily unionized industry, the same principle applies.

"The hourly people or the operators basically know more about day-to-day operations than anybody else. They know more than they've ever shared and more than they've ever been asked," says Fred Fetterolf. "When you really involve them and they understand the kind of contribution they can make, their attitude about their job, their workplace, and their employer changes dramatically."[22]

Frank Brock found out how important workers' insights can be when his company built their new factory—in response to employee complaints about the old one. Brock hired a team of top engineers to design the plant. But when the designers showed Brock their plans, Brock took the blueprints to the experts—the employees who would be cooking the candy.

"It's a fine-looking building," said one of Brock's best cooks. "But that sugar valve looks like it's about twenty feet away from the steam valve."[23]

"What's wrong with that?" asked Brock.

"Well, nothing," drawled the cook, "except that I have to have my hands on both valves at the same time."

Brock took the plans—and revisions—back to the designers. When the plant was finally built, the engineers told him that it was the smoothest start-up they'd ever seen, because the workers had helped design a facility that worked the first time out.

If organizations are to operate effectively, leadership must get into the trenches. Management reports are no match for the personal touch.

Responsibility and the Pursuit of Excellence

Not too long ago, if you did 75 percent of the things you did right, it was okay. Now, if you don't do 98 percent of those things right, some competitor will eat you for lunch.

John Spoelhof, President, Prince Corporation[24]

PEOPLE *ARE* IMPORTANT. They are any enterprise's most important asset. But that is not a license for people to do whatever they want. The workplace that focuses exclusively on meeting the individual's needs can begin to look more like an industrial mental health ward than a production center. This can be especially true in not-for-profit organizations, where lack of discipline or excellence are sometimes excused because the worker is "doing good" through the organization.

People need to have standards and be disciplined to meet them, to be motivated to do their best. That starts with the understanding that we are responsible for our behavior and for the results we achieve.

"Everyone needs a bottom line of some sort; everyone needs to be responsible, accountable to whomever it is they are serving," says Bob Buford.[25]

That is true in education, where high standards are necessary to ensure that students understand they are responsible to learn. It is true in welfare ghettos, where recipients need to learn responsibility for the consequences of their actions. And it is true on the job, where the deteriorating work habits of a generation are showing up on the bottom line.

Linda nudged her way through the crowd milling around the registration tables in the large hotel meeting room reserved for the gathering of sales representatives from Home Interiors and Gifts. As she reached out to claim her nametag, she felt all of the pressures of the recent months' return.

Since joining Home Interiors six months earlier, Linda had been on a roller coaster of highs and lows. Recruited by a friend who had been with the company several years, Linda thought she was ready for those inevitable times when sales dipped. But the last six weeks had been devastating. Her calendar of hostess parties was almost empty.

The meeting started promptly with the introduction of Barbara Hammond, vice president and national sales manager. Barbara had learned everything she knew about sales and motivation from the company's founder, Mary Crowley. From what Linda had heard, Mary Crowley was the work ethic personified.

Mary had been a twenty-one-year-old housewife with two children when her husband decided to walk out of their marriage. So with a hundred dollars in her pocket—her life savings—Mary and her children moved from Arkansas to Dallas to start a new life. With grit, brains, and optimistic tenacity, Mary began fulfilling her dream of starting her own business and eventually built Home Interiors into a $500-million-per-year industry.

In her later years, Mary Crowley became a marvelous grandmotherly figure who regularly imbued the members of Home Interiors with her own brand of optimism and self-reliance. When Mary died in 1986, Barbara Hammond picked up the mantle of Mary's personal vision for serving others through beautifying homes and helping women reach their full potential as independent sales associates.

Linda missed Barbara's introductory remarks, wondering how this cheerful woman with the sparkling eyes could maintain such poise with the pressures she must face. But Barbara Hammond had a reputation for being strong. "An iron fist in a velvet glove," one associate called her.[26]

Linda snapped out of her reverie as Barbara jolted the group with her next words.

"Some of you are feeling badly today because your sales are down. Well, I feel badly for both of us. For you ladies who are down in the dumps because things are not going well, I have ten two-letter words that will change your life if you'll act on them: *If it is to be, it is up to me.*"

Barbara paused to let the words sink in. "I take these words to heart. They apply to me as surely as they do to you. If you are to be successful, it is up to you. If you are failing, it could be that I have failed you in some way. But it is also up to you."

Linda had heard the slogan before, but today the words hit home. She knew it was all up to her. There sure wasn't anyone else in her corner. Especially not her husband Steve.

"Now I know some of you are not getting a lot of encouragement at home," the petite speaker continued, "and that hurts."

This woman's been reading my mail, Linda marveled, remembering how just yesterday Steve had asked her to cancel her trip, saying it was a waste of her time.

"Motivation is a one-to-one thing," Barbara said as she went on to tell about her own experiences as a wife, a mother, and a struggling sales associate. She stressed that success in her business depended on how well she served her customers and her family. "The greatest gift Mary Crowley gave me was when she convinced me that God made me and loved me for who I was and I could believe in myself as strongly as he believed in me. Mary told me if I failed in this business, I would fail because I didn't believe in myself. And when I say I'm going to do something, I'm responsible to do it."

Linda felt a warm flush in her cheeks. She had been working

hard, but she also knew she had blamed others for her lack of success. Sure Steve was edgy sometimes, but he had stayed up late to help her sort through orders; he had taken over some of the household duties and picked up the children from soccer practice so she could hostess parties. Maybe she should have listened more. *Barbara is right*, Linda admitted, *it's up to me.*

For Linda, this was a life-changing moment. Personal responsibility for her work was rekindled by straight talk from someone who had faced similar challenges.

"I'm not asking you to do something I haven't done," Hammond said. "I have worked every job in this company. And I am telling you that a lot of hard work and a belief in yourself and your God-given potential will pay off if you are willing to take the responsibility for the decisions you make."

Success would require personal commitment and enthusiasm for her tasks, Linda realized, whether she remained with Home Interiors, found a new line of work, or chose to be a full-time homemaker.

Many of those, like Linda, who have listened to Barbara Hammond and Mary Crowley have gone on to become highly successful business people because of that drive to take personal responsibility and then to excel. It's the same drive that compelled the two women assemblers at Cummins Engine to paint roses on each engine they assembled. Those roses were the mark of their pride in their work. Even though that mark would be covered by paint and buried under a truck hood, they were saying it was theirs.

Mary Crowley and Barbara Hammond didn't just rev up their people with peppy slogans; they gave them a vested interest by making each one an independent salesperson; they showed them how they fit into the organization and who was affected by their poor performance and how they were enriching lives with a positive performance; and finally, they placed the responsibility for each woman's performance firmly on her own shoulders. "If it is to be it is up to me" may sound like trite sloganeering, but it rings with the resounding truth that drives individuals to push their organizations to the top.

More and more women like Barbara Hammond and Mary Crowley are bringing a relationship-based work ethic from the home to the committee rooms, assembly lines, and nonprofit organizations of America. For many of America's leaders, it was in their homes that they first learned the work ethic.

———————

Ken Wessner, now retired chairman of ServiceMaster, grew up during the Depression, when a penny found under a loose chair cushion was as scarce as a full-time day job. He went through junior high school in rural Pennsylvania possessing only one shirt, which his mother would wash, dry, and iron each night. Yet Wessner does not consider his childhood as deprived.

"One of the things my parents taught me was a work ethic. It was honorable to work," he says. "Work did not bring dignity to the individual, but the individual brought dignity to the work. Along with the work ethic went the principle of discipline and responsibility practiced by our family."[27]

That principle remains with Wessner even today. He insists on a high level of work from his employees but goes out of his way to find reasons to compliment individuals on a job well done. At the same time, he never says the work is perfect. Often he points out some area that can be improved; otherwise people wouldn't have the incentive to improve. The pursuit of excellence, he believes, is an ongoing process, encouraged when people are constantly challenged to seek greater goals.

Another Pennsylvanian, Philip J. Baur, chairman of Philadelphia's Tasty Baking Company, took his family's company from the edge of ruin to a net annual sales of over $250 million. To do so he called upon attitudes learned as a child and an upbringing that stressed the importance of work.

"I just enjoyed work," says Baur. "I was brought up that way. My first job—when I was ten years old—was hoeing corn at ten cents an hour. When I got my first paycheck after sixty hours—well, that was the greatest thing in the world."[28]

Texas billionaire H. Ross Perot started breaking horses at a dollar a horse when he was six. He got a paper route when he was twelve, cutting a deal with the newspaper to more than double his commission if he began delivering papers at 3:30 in the morning—on horseback. At thirty-two he started his own company to compete head-to-head with the mega-giant IBM. On paper Perot's Electronic Data Systems made $200 million the day it went public.

When Ed Prince began his small auto parts manufacturing company in Holland, Michigan, in 1965, his goal was to build a community-based company that served its employees. In the years since, his company has grown to more than eighteen hundred employees working on a sprawling, tree-covered campus. Of the four corporate commitments distributed throughout Prince, second on the list is "promoting a culture of trust, teamwork, individual responsibility, high expectations" among his employees.

One way that commitment is fulfilled is through a pay scale based on the assumption that people need a continuing challenge. Prince has tied pay directly to performance by using a fluctuating pay scale.

For an employee's first several years, performance and pay are assessed every three months. After that time, they are reassessed every year, or at the employee's request. Based on attitude, quality and quantity of work, cooperative spirit, and adherence to basic work rules, pay rates are not only increased—they are also decreased. No sitting on the laurels of past performance; people understand they are responsible themselves and have a constant motive for improvement and excellence.

At Prince, it isn't just the line workers who labor under this "use it or lose it" philosophy. John Spoelhof, the president, applies the same commitment to his long-range planning for the company. "I don't want us to think we have it made. We have to notch up our expectations from where they are today. The Japanese expect to achieve more than we do. When we raise our expectations, we will raise our market share."[29]

When it comes to attitude and quality of work, it is up to employers to pass it on, to reinforce it in their employees. Especially the younger ones. One company that has refined this into an art is Chick-fil-A, the successful fast-food chain famous for its chicken sandwiches.

Chick-fil-A employee loyalty is no accident. "We involve ourselves with our employees, whether they are retirees or teenagers," says Gus Mir, who has owned and operated his Chick-fil-A for six years. When asked why his turnover rates are so low, he says it is not uncommon for him to meet with the parents of his youthful employees or to call them when there are problems; he adjusts schedules when a student has a major research project due; and he takes his employees on fun outings.[30]

The results are both visible and tangible. Unlike his counterparts in other fast-food chains, Gus can leave his store and trust his employees to carry on with business as usual. Because he's there for them, they are there for him; they are responsible.

And when things do go wrong, he's straightforward with them without damaging their sense of self-worth. One young employee was not measuring up, and Gus had to let him go. Six months later the young man called Gus.

"Mr. Mir, I don't know if you ever rehire kids or not, but I've tried a couple of other jobs that didn't work out. I see now what you meant by my needing to be more disciplined. I want to do better, and I really liked working for you. Will you take me back?" That young man has now been with Gus for two years and is one of his most loyal employees.

Personal responsibility and a commitment to excellence are prerequisites for any meaningful change in the way America works. Those qualities need to be instilled early, in homes, in schools, and communities. But they must also be reinforced by workplaces that take responsibility and excellence seriously.

The Value of Training

> Learning is not just a process of correcting or repairing deficiencies. We hire and promote people for what they can do, not for what they cannot do. We should encourage people to develop their gifts and maximize their strengths. Learning in the work environment should include elbow room for mistakes. In the absence of grace, there will be no reaching for potential.
>
> ServiceMaster 1990 Annual Report

THE MOST SUCCESSFUL ENTERPRISES invest the most in training their workers and equipping people to do the job. We've discovered what a difference this makes in Prison Fellowship. For years prison ministry was conducted, for the most part, by small "ma and pa" groups. Well-intentioned and deeply caring, they often started with a bang but quickly fizzled because they simply didn't know how to deal with the unique problems of prison populations.

Take the Minnesota businessman who visited an inmate every week for two years in conjunction with a Prison Fellowship visitation program. Then one Saturday morning the inmate appeared on the man's doorstep. He had been released from prison and had nowhere to go.

"Come in, friend," the businessman said, throwing his arms around the man. "Make yourself at home."

The businessman then explained that his wife was away and that he was leaving on a hunting trip, but would return on Monday. In the meantime, he told the offender, use the house and the family car (a Lincoln) and "relax, have a good time."

The ex-convict—out of prison all of three hours—did just that. The businessman returned home on Monday to find his car wrecked and his friend back in jail.

Today the more than forty thousand volunteers of Prison Fellowship are not allowed into prisons until they have completed twenty hours of training; after that there are continuing programs, some very professional and detailed. And, yes, on the training agenda is what to do when an ex-inmate comes and knocks on your door. Our businessman friend remains today a great volunteer; he's had on-the-job training.

But training does more than just equip. It sends a message to workers that says: We want you to do well. We care.

Training is also closely linked to those tribal goals and corporate values that drive a company. In ServiceMaster's case, training maintenance people means not just showing them how to clean tough spots, but how their cleaning work advances the goals and visions of the institutions they serve. And that can pay great dividends, as ServiceMaster's Ken Wessner knows from personal experience.

Like Brock, DePree, and the other successful leaders we've interviewed, Ken Wessner knows the importance of hands-on management: he visits clients regularly, talks to employees, and finds out firsthand both the employees' needs and the skills required for the job.

As an example, Wessner tells of the municipal hospital he visited a month after ServiceMaster took over the maintenance contract. Built shortly after the turn of the century, the hospital had been transformed from a small sixty-bed institution to a six-hundred bed hospital providing a regional trauma center and nuclear medicine facility.[31]

"We are flattered that ServiceMaster's chairman of the board would come personally to consummate a contract with our hospital," said Dr. Underwood, the chief of staff.

"I'm pleased to be invited. It's not often I get the chance to see one of these fine older institutions."

"You mean relics," Underwood said, pointing to the high plastered walls and arched windows. "Your maintenance people will love keeping this old thing clean."

"Your maintenance people, Doctor, not mine," Ken replied, reminding his client of ServiceMaster's policy to maintain existing personnel whenever possible.

"Yes, well," the physician stammered awkwardly, "you may get some questions from our professional staff about that." He emphasized "professional" as he led Wessner into the boardroom, where more than two dozen physicians, head nurses, and administrative managers had gathered to meet him. *And grill me,* thought Wessner.

Wessner's appearance serves him well in situations like this. Although soft-spoken, he stands tall and erect, distinguished by angular features, a broad forehead, and prematurely white hair. His bifocaled, gold-rimmed glasses add a scholarly touch, but do not hide the warmth and wisdom in his blue eyes.

"Ours is a very complicated business that appears deceptively simple," Wessner began as he addressed the group. "Some may regard the cleaning business as menial and beneath them. But at ServiceMaster the housekeeper, window washer, or floor finisher is just as important as the Ph.D. we employ to research and develop products. We begin each new contract with the belief that every individual's work is valuable and dignifying. That's why we try to maintain the current staff. It's also why I asked to meet with you today, before I meet with the staff."

Curious glances ricocheted around the table until a surgeon broke the silence. "What do we have to do with how you clean the buildings?"

"Well, you will help us train," Wessner said. "We have put a great deal of thought into our training programs. We want our employees' lives enriched by what they do each day. To do that we need your help."

"I don't think my colleagues understand what it is we are to do," said Dr. Underwood.

"Each month we hold Housekeeping Councils for our employees. This is a thirty to forty-five minute training session where every employee is briefed on various aspects of hospital operations. For example, I hear you have some new radiology equipment here. We would ask one of you to come in and explain how the equipment is used generally, who it helps, and how it helps them."

"Do you expect janitors to understand radiology?" asked one of the radiologists.

"No, but we do expect them to be able to see the important part they play in the mission of the hospital and its various functions. It connects them to a greater goal and inspires commitment to quality, cleanliness, and even to those of you on the professional staff."

After this meeting, Wessner asked to meet the maintenance employees.

"I didn't know you wanted a special meeting, Mr. Wessner," said the supervisor.

"Oh, I don't want a group meeting. Let's just walk around and talk with the employees," said Wessner who knows the meaning of walking and talking in the trenches.

Wessner and the supervisor strolled up and down the corridors, moving in and out of storerooms, utility rooms, and patient rooms, chatting amiably with the maintenance staff. Along the way Wessner was briefed on individual employees. One in particular was what the supervisor called, "a problem employee."

"Ellis is a nice guy but a very slow window washer, and a complainer. I don't think he'll last." That was all the challenge Wessner needed.

They found Ellis on the ground floor of the old wing with a squeegee in his right hand, supporting it at the wrist with the other.

Ellis was a tall, wiry black man whose short-cropped hair was beginning to gray on the sides.

"Nice to meet you, Ellis," Wessner said and shook hands as Ellis's boss introduced them. "Say, are these older windows harder to clean?"

"Mr. Wessner, they're all hard to clean for me," Ellis said with a short laugh and a shake of his head.

"Why's that?" Wessner asked.

"It's my arm, sir. See, I had this accident a few years back. Messed up my hand awful."

Ellis unbuttoned the cuff of his blue shirt as he described his accident and the subsequent surgery. He showed a large scar, and with a bony finger traced its twisted path across the palm of his hand, around his thumb, and up his wrist. Wessner could easily see that the injury would impede Ellis's performance.

"When I put pressure on this squeegee, whoa mercy, a shootin' pain runs up my arm all the way to my shoulder blades."

"Ellis, do you like being a window washer?" Wessner asked.

The man paused anxiously before answering. "No sir, Mr. Wessner, I can't say that I do."

"Then why are you doing it?"

"It's the only job I got. I was on the loadin' docks fifteen years before my accident. My back's still strong, but I can't lift much of nothin'." He rubbed his right wrist self-consciously.

"Ellis, how would you like to be trained to be a floor finisher?"

"Sure! I mean I guess so. You reckon somethin' heavy like that would strain my arm?"

"It doesn't strain mine."

"You mean you're a floor finisher, Mr. Wessner?"

"Ellis, I've done every job any worker in this hospital does. Now how about that training program? Interested?"

"Yes, sir!" Ellis beamed, "I sure am."

Ellis was in the first training program for floor finishers at the hospital and was soon the best floor finisher and fastest learner on staff. He was promoted to trainer, taking great pride in his work and training others. When Wessner first met Ellis, the man's uniform was dirty and his general appearance sloppy. After Wessner showed a personal interest in him, Ellis started coming to work in freshly washed, starched uniforms. He began looking like the professionally skilled worker he was.

ServiceMaster has a leader-led training philosophy that requires all management personnel to individually train for and perform every maintenance function, while employees team up alongside those with whom they work at the contract site to observe them. The payoff is an invigorated workplace where costly turnover is low and worker morale high.

Since people's abilities and skills are not static, ServiceMaster is also committed to lifelong training. "Because when you stop training your people," Wessner says, "they don't just stay the same. Through apathy and boredom, they actually regress."

Ellis's story is not just about the importance of training, however. It is about bringing a company's values right down to the workers; it is about valuing each employee as an individual; it is about getting out of the executive suite and onto the floor and managing from the trenches; and it is about giving each worker a chance to do his or her best.

David Kearns, former CEO of Xerox Corporation, known as the father of Xerox's now-famous training programs, believes training must begin from the top down.

"At Xerox we said we're going to give everybody all the information they need and not reserve it for different layers of management, and we're going to train everybody. We started training from the top down because our employees were skeptical about whether top management really knew what they were doing. It was 'they' and 'us.' It took three years to train a hundred thousand people, but that training really motivated and made a change."[32]

Often training takes the form of close mentoring-type relationships between young employees and their supervisors. Skills might be taught in seminars and training programs, but

organization values, like family values, are often passed generation to generation.

Bill Burnson didn't look like a slave driver, thought Don, as he
watched the older man run a long-handled dust mop over the reception area floor at the Eckerd Drugs in Seminole Mall. More like
an animated George Goebel, cracking dour little jokes with sting-
ers on the end. But Don could see this was going to be a long day.[33]

A recent graduate from pharmacy school, Don had just joined
Eckerd's management program and was a little apprehensive. He
lacked experience with over-the-counter health and beauty aids, but
that was no big deal. He had worked at a hospital pharmacy his last
year in school; a retail store couldn't be that much different. But
Burnson? Don had been warned about Bill's reputation for driving
manager trainees hard.

By noon, Don wished the day was over. He and Bill had filled
more than a hundred prescriptions, Bill had whisked through the
reception area twice with his long-handled mop, and the young
trainee had handled an employee check-out at the cosmetics
counter while Jane, the cosmetics clerk, talked to an elderly blue-
haired lady about hair coloring. In the midst of the maelstrom, Bill
dispensed a litany of over-the-counter wisdom to his new disciple.

"Clerks like Jane are the backbone of this company," he told
Don over lunch. "They see the customers, talk to them. Find out
what they like and don't like. Make them feel better about their
ailments. Wish 'em a nice day. That sort of thing. And on the rare
occasion they need a prescription filled, they're more likely to come
here instead of the competition. Without our Janies, you and I
would be on the street."

By the end of the day, Don was bone tired. As they were
cleaning up before the relief pharmacist arrived, Bill took Don aside
and asked him if he was interested in getting ahead at Eckerd.

"Sure," Don said, thinking he'd finally hear something about
the real power structure at Eckerd Drugs.

"Well, then, you're going to have to work longer and harder than anyone else. You'll have to do things they didn't teach you in pharmacy school—like covering for a sick employee, juggling work schedules for yourself and everybody else, listening to customers, getting to know them, caring for your employees. . . ." The list went on and on.

"Eckerd helped make my life meaningful," Bill said. "Thanks to the stock Eckerd Drugs has given me, I was able to get my daughter through medical school. I owe this company a lot."

Don, coached by his mentor, went on to become a successful Eckerd manager and passed this same ethic on to others.

Leader-led training and mentoring provide an opportunity to encourage corporate values, while the close relationship gives management a chance to spot troublesome attitudes and practices and nip them in the bud.

True value is not just the worth of things. It is not just an appreciation of tangible assets tallied on a balance sheet. It is also the value of people, the worth of their individuality. A well-trained, enriched, and empowered work force is the direct link between true productivity and true profit.

Dollars and Sense

When we started the quality process at Xerox, we said there were three things that we needed to do. We had to improve customer satisfaction; we had to improve market share; and we had to improve our profits. We printed up these little cards that stated the values of the company and what we were doing. Everybody carries these cards around, and now you can go to anybody in the company and say, "What's your share of customer satisfaction? How do you get measured on that? And what's your share of profit improvement?" So any employee can say, "This is my piece of that this year." Everybody feels that they know exactly what their part of the action is."

David Kearns[34]

LEST YOU THINK WE HAVE BEEN talking only about ivory tower principles that might motivate people because they appeal to their nobler instincts, let's be practical. Let's talk profit. The fact of the matter is that people work not only for a sense of achievement, but also for personal gain. The profit motive and good competition drive individuals in the same way they drive corporations, and workers have a right to expect a return on every effort they invest in a company.

What we saw in the Soviet Union would convince anyone that the abandonment of the profit motive and competition is a sure prescription for disaster. It is evident in the fact that nothing works and no one cares; their farm-run communes are falling apart despite rich soil and abundant resources; their economy is in chaos.

Why? Because no one has any personal incentive to work.

When workers are given a stake in a company's success, it changes the whole character of the business. As Jack Reichert discovered when he gave out stock in Brunswick, despite the opposition of a lot of stockholders, the morale and motivation of his employees changed. "People take care of a business they own," he says.

Jack Eckerd found exactly the same thing. His employees, like Bill Burnson, were fiercely loyal. Why? Because they felt it was *their* company.

One can tell almost from the first encounter when employees have a stake in the enterprise.

"I was in Home Depot the other day just wandering around," says Ross Perot, speaking of the nation's largest do-it-yourself warehouse chain, which trains its employees to give construction advice and person-to-person encouragement for the do-it-yourself homeowner. "Every employee I encountered was determined to sell me something. They're stockholders. And when I asked if they were stockholders, they said 'Yes sir,' and they had the numbers. You go into Sam Walton's Wal-Mart stores and you get the same thing. It goes back to the direct contact he has with the people who do the work and recognition of their efforts."[35]

Ed Noble, former director of the federal government's Synthetic Fuel Corporation, is a successful oil man, developer, and entrepreneur. "In every company I've operated," he says, "I've had profit sharing with every employee after they've been there a year. My key executives had a percentage of the profits based on earnings. Every employee had a matching bonus based on profits. I found it motivates the people all along the line."[36]

But incentives are not limited to stock options. Principles as simple as linking executive salaries to the company's performance or linking executive salaries to workers' salaries send an important message of equity and fairness. Workers become justifiably outraged when they are denied raises because the company is losing money while top management still gets huge salaries and bonuses. Incentives have to be fair and go from top to bottom.

Heads-up business people eliminate such double standards in the workplace and reward employee efforts with dignity and respect. Alcoa's Fred Fetterolf is one who recognizes the importance of this.

———

Alcoa's management team had been cooped up for more than a hundred hours sorting out goals and objectives for their company. Often, values were more easily written down than carried out. As O'Neill and Fetterolf worked with their team, it became increasingly apparent that valuing one's workers—one of their primary goals—might mean dollar values as well.

"We will have to fight for the hearts and minds of our employees to overcome ninety years of history," Fetterolf suggested, "and do things another way."[37]

"Like what?"

"Like getting rid of privileges and perks that emphasize the differences between 'us and them,'" said a senior vice president.

"Like reserved parking at the plants for managers and executives."

"And two types of cafeterias," contributed another.

"If we are working against the same standards and toward the same goals, we ought to make sure that employee pay and benefits reflect the individual's part in making that happen," said Fetterolf.

"Not equal pay, but equal standards of pay," O'Neill added.

"That raises an interesting point about profit sharing and bonuses," said the personnel officer. "For example, our twenty-five-year service award for salaried employees is a higher percentage than it is for the hourly workers."

"Change it!" O'Neill snapped.

"And we have no savings plan for our hourly people."

"We'll change that, too."

In the course of the meeting the Alcoa team agreed to include profitability and competition as core values. As O'Neill puts it, "It's the backbone of why any enterprise exists in the first place. To make a profit. It is what empowers the individual to work in the first place. The worker must see himself as advancing, achieving, moving ahead. And it's not always just monetary profitability. It's more fundamentally human than that."

As a result, Alcoa's workers now see how their work, their participation in production, in decision making, and in problem solving not only makes Alcoa more profitable as a company, but also benefits the employees both financially and in terms of human growth.

The incentive motive both as a moral and pragmatic principle, is an essential ingredient in the work ethic. Properly applied it is the glue that bonds workers to the workplace. The fruit of our labors not only pays the bills, it also encourages our growth as human beings.

For Max DePree and Herman Miller the moral aspects weigh heavily on the company's top chief executives. For example, the CEO's earnings were capped at twenty times the earnings of the average worker. We support such a cap, in principle (although we certainly make no claim to what is a fair multiple for every industry). Such a policy overcomes the gross inequities created by executive excesses, so prominent in the eighties, which abuse the system and create deep resentment. More importantly, as the average worker sees that when CEO's earnings go up, theirs go up proportionately, they *believe*—correctly—that they are valued by management.

The profit motive is strong in America, as well it should be. It is the backbone of the free enterprise system. It is also a moral imperative that carries moral responsibility. And it goes beyond compensating employees.

Philip Baur never expected to find himself at the top of a multimillion dollar enterprise. But when this unassuming man took over his family's bakery company in 1982, it was in trouble. They had lost 25 percent of their business in recent years and were $18 million in debt. Baur's brother-in-law, who had been running the company since the death of Baur's father, insisted on borrowing more money each year to pay a dividend to stockholders. Now most of the company's top executives were resigning in protest. Phil knew he had to take control of the company.

A year after he did, Tasty Baking had developed a new strategic plan based on a set of core values and was slowly working its way up. At that point the company's new president, Nelson Harris, suggested to Baur, now chairman of the company, that he should take the company private again with a leveraged buy out.

Baur agreed that it would be a shrewd move. "But to do that we would have to buy out our stockholders at today's lower rate. We both know we couldn't live with ourselves if we didn't give the stockholders who have stayed with us during these lean years an opportunity to reap the rewards when Tasty Baking turns around again."[38]

The issue was settled. Tasty Baking Company would not return to private ownership. How we profit is just as important as how much we profit.

As Paul O'Neill of Alcoa points out, we must expand our definition of profit. Profit is a paycheck, benefits, stock options, and bonuses. But it is also the dignity received from a job done well, training that builds individual skills and enriches lives, the camaraderie and sense of belonging that comes from working toward a common goal alongside others, and a belief that society is better off because we went to work today.

A workplace that produces profits on balance sheets and in the lives of workers cannot be achieved by a mechanical manipulation of these principles. It requires leadership to make it happen. Whether in big companies or in small enterprises, in civic work or volunteer groups, in our families or with our friends, all of us at times find ourselves in a position to lead others. The question is how.

Working to Serve

Business is not just doing deals; business is having great products, doing great engineering, and providing tremendous service to customers. Finally, business is a cobweb of human relationships.

H. Ross Perot[39]

Valuing workers. Managing from the trenches. Communicating. Inspiring excellence. Training. Using profits to motivate. These are all strategies that empower workers to drive their companies to the top. But it is only leaders who can give workers that power.

When we say leaders, we do not mean the highly paid, media moguls, celebrity athletes and performers, or get-rich-quick business barons with their rich-and-famous lifestyles. The leadership that will bring America to greater productivity and lead to a restored work ethic is the leadership that begins with a very old notion: doing our very best for others.

This kind of servant leadership does not develop overnight. It emerges out of the life of the leader as he or she responds to the changes in the workplace.

Byron Oliver is president of CIGNA's Group Pension Division, which manages billions of dollars in pension funds for companies all over the world. Each year at his division's headquarters in Hartford, Connecticut, row after row of work stations fill with pressured intensity as accountants, customer service workers, and account managers assemble the documentation their client companies need to prepare and file the taxes related to their pension programs. During Plan Year, as the process is called, Oliver and his associates must accomplish what amounts to six months of work in the first three months of the year.[40]

When Oliver and the other top management personnel have completed the initial phase and passed mounds of paperwork on to other employees for the final stages, thousands of hours of work still remain, which means twelve-hour days, seven days a week for the next month. Last year, Oliver decided he could not just sit on his hands while others worked even though, technically, his part was done. If his company was going to get through Plan Year, then everyone had to jump in and do whatever it took, so he decided to let his people know that he was behind them.

"Dot, get a memo out this afternoon to the executive staff," he said. "Tell them that we will be serving coffee and refreshments in the production areas on a regular basis throughout the day, every day, until Plan Year is finished."

"Shall I call a caterer, sir?"

"No caterers. We'll do the serving ourselves. Me. You. The vice presidents, and senior account managers."

Over the next few weeks, Oliver and his division's top management pushed carts from one office to another. And in exchange for coffee, donuts, and a little encouragement they got a lot of information. Employees were tired, some were not working hard, others were discouraged by the significant increase in the workload this year.

"Coffee, Charlene?" Oliver asked the startled customer service coordinator just as she finished one of the scores of calls listed on her computer screen.

"Excuse me?" Charlene stammered, caught off guard by the boss's presence in his rolled-up shirt sleeves.

"Coffee. Cream or sugar?" he joked. "I'm in training for the airlines!"

"Well, thank you, Mr. Oliver," she said, reaching for the styrofoam cup.

"Thank *you*, Charlene. By the way, how are things going?"

As she sipped her coffee, she showed Oliver what she was doing, explaining that customers were often confused by their statements.

"I don't know who designed them, but I can bet they hadn't talked to many customers. If it doesn't look like a bank statement, they don't understand it."

Later at a management meeting, Oliver explained what the customer service coordinator had told him. "What are you learning out there by the way?" he asked.

Without a pause, one manager after another began a litany of their findings. Some things were tough to hear and even tougher to solve, but underneath it was an air of optimism.

"Here's what I've learned," Oliver began after each manager had spoken. "I've learned how foolish I am." He went on to explain that as he walked around with his pushcart, he saw that he had been operating with an upside-down organizational model. Oliver's experiment in servant leadership had made him a convert to management in the trenches as well.

"I don't know where this came from, but whoever said senior management was to do all the thinking; middle management, the controlling and communicating; and folks on the front line, the doing, was dead wrong!"

Nods and grunts of agreement echoed around the table.

"Folks, our job as senior management is to do the doing, providing the environment and the resources for the front lines to do the thinking. Middle management should do the serving and training. And I see some real training needs out there."

Oliver and his associates commissioned a panel of employees to recommend how to improve customer service. The panel came up with a way to eliminate what was a staggering 15 percent error factor in customer statements. Since the errors were primarily careless mistakes, their long-range plan was to institute a training program; in the meantime, though, workers would double up, checking each other.

The plan reduced the 15 percent error rate to one-tenth of 1 percent in a short time, as two people working on the same account created healthy competition. Neither one wanted to be the person with the wrong answer! They also did the calculations faster. Worker output doubled. And no customer complaints!

"The best piece of advice we got from the employee panel," says one executive, "was to reduce the division's strategy to one page and distribute it to all employees." The company disseminated their group mission in memos, plaques, and cards throughout the division.

CIGNA also learned that they had misjudged the employees' interest in the company.

Each year the division held a results meeting for managers and supervisors; employees were not invited to attend. But this year the employees asked to be included.

The next annual results meeting was held in a local theater, filled with eager, interested, employees. At the meeting, management introduced a slide show honoring the division's "heroes," those employees who characterized the values of the company through their lives and in their work.

It was just the beginning. As Oliver served in the trenches, he learned just what it was that his people needed to do their best: a sense of the company's values and vision, and a stake in its success; motivation and opportunity to do flawless work; and an opportunity to show management what they knew about the business.

Sometimes "servant leadership" will demand sacrifice on the part of leaders. Andrew Barnes, editor of the *St. Petersburg Times*, one of America's leading newspapers, believes this type of leadership must begin with the CEO or even with the board of directors. When the *Times* faced a hostile takeover by the billionaire Bass brothers from Texas in 1989, Martha Poynter—longtime trustee and heir of the founding family—was offered $36 million for her share in the paper. Since she believed the value of local ownership was greater than increasing her own personal wealth, Mrs. Poynter sold her stock to the *Times* instead—for much less than the Bass brothers offered. She put the interests of those she was responsible for ahead of her own—a rare quality in today's egocentric culture.[41]

When Frank Brock left the Brock Candy Company, it was due to a personal conviction. He believed that education was in trouble and that college students today were being taught facts almost devoid of values. So he accepted the position of director of marketing at Covenant College, a Christian school in his hometown of Lookout Mountain, Georgia. The principles he learned in business made just as much sense in an academic setting, and Frank stepped right into the trenches to find out how he could serve the students who were his primary responsibility.[42]

"What is it you like about this school?" Frank asked a coed one day in the large lobby where students regularly gathered just to hang out.

"I can tell you what I don't like," she responded quickly. "There's no place to sit here in the lounge."

Frank had to agree. The large lobby was almost bare.

Later that week the college president asked Frank for his suggestions on a new promotional package for Covenant's student recruitment program.

"These plans look great. That four-color brochure and the new video are well done," Frank told him, "but you're wasting your money."

"What?" said the startled administrator.

"What do you want the potential students to do after they see the brochure or the video?"

"Come to campus and look us over," the president replied.

"And what will they do when they get here?"

"Look at our facilities. Talk to students. Recruitment has the whole thing tightly planned," he responded defensively.

"Well if they talk to students, they'll find some pretty unhappy campers. We've been promising them a redecorated lobby for six months. I know it's a small thing and the school has a tight budget, but the kids are irate. That will be passed along to your potential recruits."

"So what do you suggest? You know we can't afford to redecorate right now," the president said, reminding Frank of his role as the school's fund-raiser.

"Take the chairs out of your office and put them in the student lounge. And ask every other administrator to do the same," Frank proposed boldly.

"You're out of your mind. Those kids will destroy the furniture."

"I think you're wrong. But what if you're not? Are students the reason this school exists or undamaged furniture?"

At the daily chapel service the following day, the president announced his decision to move chairs and sofas from the administration offices into the lobby until the school could afford new furniture. "And young people," he pleaded, "please take care of it. We cannot afford new furniture for both of us."

A cheer went up from the student body, followed by a standing ovation for the beaming president.

A simple principle—putting your best resources at the disposal of those who need them—is at the heart of servant leadership.

The principle of putting those you lead first could come naturally to anyone who has served in the field in the military. Chuck remembers well a lesson learned when he was a Marine second lieutenant.

Back on the base or on board ship, there is a strict line drawn between enlisted men and officers. The officers eat in their own mess or in the ship's wardroom. But in the field there's one inviolable rule: no officer, from the general to a lieutenant, is served until all the troops have been served.

Leaders lead by serving their employees and their communities.

For Byron Oliver, servant leadership often means community service. At three o'clock each Thursday afternoon, thirty fourth and fifth graders stampede into CIGNA's Group Pension headquarters as part of a mentoring program sponsored by Hartford's school system. The inner-city youngsters are linked up in one-to-one mentoring sessions with CIGNA's executive staff, including the president.

In the midst of a busy schedule, Oliver rarely misses these sessions. "When you get involved with some of the community's problems," he says, "it makes you a better representative of your company, and directly or indirectly it's going to help make you a better manager and a better person."[43]

The Fieldstone Foundation, which Peter Ochs set up, channels donations to humanitarian causes, local community and education projects, cultural concerns, and Christian ministries. His employees share a piece of this action, too. Any Fieldstone employee can give a hundred dollars a year of company money to any cause by filling out a check requisition. The company also matches dollar for dollar the contributions their employees personally make to charitable causes, up to a thousand dollars per year per employee.

Few will argue that more of this new type of leader and worker are needed if the American workplace is to be strengthened to meet the challenge of the fast-approaching twenty-first century. And few will contest that the leadership that changed history took the form of a servant. He met his followers where they were: fishermen, tax collectors, educators, women artisans, and homemakers and showed them their potential as contributing human beings.

———

These six principles—the value of the worker, walking and talking in the trenches, responsibility and the pursuit of excellence, the value of training, dollars and sense, and working to serve— sound simple enough, but if applied sincerely they can revolutionize the workplace in America.

These principles go to the very heart of the modern American dilemma: the sense of alienation and isolation. In our highly technological, impersonal society people feel lonely, helpless, unable to change the circumstances of their lives. They give up, drawing into a shell of cynicism and despair.

Pollsters have uncovered widespread skepticism about almost every area of life: only 50 percent of those eligible vote, and this percentage has been steadily declining; and in the area of work, 45 percent believe that hard work no longer pays off, and that percentage is even higher among those earning less than $20,000 per year.

This is what the revolution has done to us: It has stripped us of our spiritual roots from which we get our sense of individual significance, purpose, and God-given dignity.

Now restoring this sense of significance, overcoming the alienation and cynicism is not going to be accomplished by presidential proclamation or self-esteem commissions that so many states are ludicrously establishing, nor by new labor-management agreements or policy manuals. But these attitudes can be changed when we regain our sense of respect for the dignity of the individual—when we recover what the revolution stripped away from us.

These principles, if practiced in the workplace and within all human relationships, would begin that process. They are the key to not only reviving the sagging work ethic, but to restoring civility, community, decency, and trust in our society.

In Conclusion

The world is moved along not only by the mighty shoves of its heroes, but also by the agreggate of the tiny pushes of each honest worker.

Helen Keller

THE STORY IS TOLD OF A MAN WHO visited a stone quarry and asked three of the workers what they were doing.

"Can't you see?" said the first one irritably. "I'm cutting a stone."

The second replied, "I'm earning a hundred pounds a week."

But the third put down his pick and thrust out his chest proudly. "I'm building a cathedral," he said.[1]

People view work in many ways: as a necessary evil to keep bread on the table; as a means to a sizable bank account; as self-fulfillment and identity; as an economic obligation within society; as a means to a life of leisure.

Yet none of these represents an adequate view of work that provides ongoing or complete satisfaction for our labors. We are more than material beings, more than social beings, and more than cogs in the machinery of work.

We are, above all, spiritual beings, and as such we need to rediscover the moral and spiritual significance for every area and aspect of our lives, including our work.

Why, then, should we work?

Because work gives expression to our creative gifts and thus fulfills our need for meaning and purpose.

Because work is intrinsically good when done with the proper attitude and motive.

Because we are commanded to exercise stewardship over the earth, participating in the work of Creation in a way that glorifies God.

Because we are citizens of this earth and have certain responsibilities to our fellow citizens.

It is this moral character of work that historically has been the very heart of the work ethic.

When people finish reading a book, they often put it down and say, "Wasn't that interesting," or, "I enjoyed that."

Well, if that's your response, we've missed the mark. Actually we hoped to make you as angry as we are, to prompt you to go out and make things happen.

We told you at the beginning that this would not be just another hand-wringing diatribe, but a call to action with specific suggestions for things we can do.

We *can* make a difference.

Why not begin in our own homes and families by instilling the kind of values we've been talking about in our children or encouraging them in our grandchildren? If you don't have children, how about being a big brother or sister or a foster grandparent or taking on one of the similar roles available through volunteer agencies that link you up with young people who have no family.

Start banging on the doors of your school board; go to their meetings—maybe even run for the school board; examine the curriculum; ask about tests and standards and what values are being taught—or not being taught—in your local school system. We pay the taxes; so let's demand accountability.

Lobby for choice in education. If Polly Williams could make a difference in Milwaukee, we can make a difference in our own towns. Visit your local legislators and call your senator or congressman. Tell them you want choice in education, voucher systems, and standards.

And while you're at it, tell them you're tired of paying taxes to keep people idle on welfare and in prisons. Politicians aren't going to act until an outraged citizenry demands change. And if you aren't outraged, you should be.

Write to the editor of your paper. All of us have some forum where we can let our opinions be known, be it a Rotary Club, a garden club, a prayer group, or our cronies on the golf course. Or suggest a good book on the work ethic and business ethics in a book study group or Sunday school class. Just don't sit back and wait for Joe or Alice to do it.

And finally, start applying the principles we presented in chapter 12, no matter what your vocation or calling. Practice these principles in your own life and work, and you will begin to affect the lives of those you come in contact with, whether you're a CEO, a homemaker, a teacher, a bag boy at the supermarket, a secretary, an electrician, a school bus driver—well, the list is endless, of course.

Why doesn't America work? Because for too long too many of us have waited for someone else to do something. Change starts with us.

But we haven't a moment to waste. We're squandering our most precious assets.

Can we make America work—restore our productiveness and competitive place in the world, raise responsible young people, and clean up the mess in our inner cities and prisons?

Yes. Emphatically yes. But make no mistake: The key is to restore a high and morally rooted view of work that once again inculcates in the American character those historic virtues of the work ethic—industry, thrift, respect for property, pride in craft, and concern for community.

We started this book with the true story of a prison where people were driven mad by lack of meaningful work. Now let us take you to a prison where the principles we've discussed have been applied, and where the people are anything but mad.

Humaita is located in San Jose dos Campos, Brazil, a relatively prosperous city of six hundred thousand in the heart of the country's industrial belt. Like the United States, Brazil is known for its overcrowded prison system. But the brutality of Brazil's prisons is second to none.

In 1972 when Dr. Silvio Marques Neto, the judge assigned to San Jose, saw the appalling conditions in Humaita, he tried to close the facility. Then two men, Mario Ottoboni, a genial, round-faced lawyer, and Hugo Veronese, a psychologist and professor, convinced the judge that reform was possible. Ottoboni and Veronese believed that a prison could be run humanely and securely on Christian principles and offered a plan to take over Humaita. Officials were understandably skeptical, but the men persisted; having nothing to lose, the officials gave in. Soon Ottoboni, Veronese, and Neto were busily reorganizing a part of the prison; in 1982 they took over the entire institution.

Today the white-walled building next to the police station in the center of San Jose dos Campos does not look like a prison, and it certainly doesn't look like a former torture chamber.

We entered through a courtyard where patches of flowers spread color against whitewashed walls. Even the steel-barred gates have a polished sheen, and the floors sparkle. There is none of the acrid odor we have come to expect in prisons.

"When a prisoner comes to Humaita," explained Mario Ottoboni, "the first thing we do is tell him that he is important to us as an individual and that he will have the opportunity to earn our trust. Restoring his human dignity, giving him hope for the future, is our first priority, whether he's a convicted murderer or a compulsive thief."

Mario showed us through his two offices, deliberately located on opposite sides of the prison—one near the front, and one in the maximum security area. Having an office in both areas requires him to walk often through the prison, see the inmates, and hear what they are thinking. He frequently modifies policies at the inmates' recommendations.

Everywhere we went in the prison we saw evidence of a healthy work ethic. Whether it was cleaning and painting the facility, planning and scheduling work in the craft shop, or working outside of the prison, every inmate was busily engaged in meaningful work.

Inmates at Humaita, when proven trustworthy, are involved in every aspect of the administration, maintenance, and even security of the facility. Long-time inmates are responsible for escorting newer inmates to outside appointments. There is no guarantee that the inmate will not try to escape, but Mario and the others have fostered such a strong sense of responsibility that inmates watch out for one another. Escapes are rare.

Volunteers play a vital role at Humaita. Many of them act as surrogate parents. "Godparents" adopt an inmate as a godson and actually assimilate him into their lives as if he were their own. All of the training courses and the assistance to inmates are provided by volunteers—a message which is not lost on those in the prison. They realize that these people are not helping them because they have to, but because they want to.

Along with the training that is basic to the mentoring program between volunteers and inmates, inmates are offered a series of voluntary classes that cover everything from fine arts, to job skills, to literacy. There is also a required series of "valorization" classes, which seek to instill values and character into inmates from the first day they enter Humaita. Voluntary Bible studies and services are also conducted regularly.

Management in the trenches—or in the prison yards; personal responsibility for excellence and behavior; training; servanthood of volunteers and brother inmates; the dignity of the individual. It seemed almost too good to be true, and frankly we were a bit skeptical.

We talked to scores of people inside and outside the prison, defenders and detractors alike. No one—even those law enforcement officials who thought torture was needed for Brazil's inmates, or the well-meaning folks who thought inmates were worked too hard—said that Humaita was anything other than what it seemed to be. And it all boiled down to one inescapable conclusion: At Humaita, lives really were being changed. While 75 percent of Brazilian prisoners re-offend after release, only 4 percent of those from Humaita do.

As we were preparing to leave, we saw two areas of the prison that may explain better than anything else what makes Humaita work.

The first was the dreaded punishment chamber. One of our guides led us to the end of a long corridor and swung open the door. When we looked inside, however, we discovered that the solitary cell was no longer a place of terror where men were tortured. It had been converted into a small chapel. We saw a table with freshly cut flowers on it, some chairs, and on the wall a beautiful carving of Christ on the cross.

"He's the one doing the time for us," one inmate told us, pointing to the cross. "That's why we come here to pray." Over the cross were the words *Estamos juntos*—"We are together."

Nothing could more dramatically capture the spirit of Humaita, or the message we've attempted to convey in this book. Not guards versus inmates, bosses versus workers, but all working together to give human dignity and moral purpose to life.

Then as we were walking toward the gate, we paused just

outside the craft shop in front of another huge sign painted on the wall, a daily reminder of an enduring truth for the residents of Humaita. We wished we could bring it home with us and post it over the doors of every factory and every schoolroom, hang it in every home—probably over the television—and on every street corner in America.

The sign read: *Quem vive matando tempo acaba morrendo junto*—"He who lives by killing time dies with it."

With Gratitude

When in the spring of 1990 we decided to write this book, we set some rather modest goals. Both of us had traveled around the globe, seen hundreds of prisons—one of us had even spent time in one—and we shared deep convictions about the need to provide meaningful work in American prisons, factories behind walls, as Chief Justice Warren Burger so well described it. So prison reform was high on our agenda.

We also believed that in the face of America's evident decline in world markets we might, based on Jack's extensive business experience, have some perspectives and ideas to offer.

Well, now that you have read this book, you will recognize that the job proved to be much more formidable than we expected. In looking at the work ethic, we found it necessary to search out its historical roots as well as its far-reaching implications in the welfare culture and education—a big research task involving fascinating and important information. And rather than draw on one man's experience in the business world, we decided to survey others; that meant interviewing business leaders in every walk of life—twenty-eight in all. Tackling such an immense subject over the course of one year would have been impossible but for the fact that we were so ably assisted. We are indebted to many.

First among them is Judith Markham with whom Chuck has worked since 1983 on four books. She lived up to her reputation as a premier editor in the profession. Judith is patient (through twelve drafts—literally), persevering, creative, and a joy to work with. Equally important has been Jim Roberts, Jack's executive assistant for more than four years, who conducted some of the interviews, drafted several business sections, and coordinated our marketing and publicity programs with the publisher.

Chuck's assistant, Deborah Kinnaird, along with Jim, shouldered much of the heavy load. Deborah drafted, coordinated research, and worked closely with Judith in the editing process.

We are grateful as well to Nelson Keener, a Prison Fellowship senior vice president, who handled contract negotiations and a myriad of administrative chores; to T. M. Moore, president of Chesapeake Seminary and a scholar of the first rank, for his contributions to the historical sections of the book; to Tom Crawford, Kimon Sargeant, and John Butin, from Justice Fellowship, whose exhaustive research provided background material; to Dr. Daryl Charles of Prison Fellowship for much research help throughout; to Kathleen Corcoran for an exhaustive job of fact checking and proofing; to Margaret Shannon, an old Colson friend, for invaluable research at the Library of Congress; and to Mike Gerson, aide to Senator Dan Coats, who assisted with research, some drafting, and a very helpful critique; to Grace McCrane and Nancy Niemeyer, Chuck's faithful secretaries, for deciphering his handwriting (it is a very select fraternity that can do that) and for working over draft after draft in word processing; to Donna Varnam who faxed hundreds of pages of text back and forth; and to Judy Lowery, Beth Marshall, and Marilyn Downs of Jack's personal staff who helped similarly with Jack's material.

We especially appreciate the time given us by many corporate leaders. Each one made a very special contribution, and much of the wisdom reflected in these pages came from those interviews.

Jack conducted interviews with: Andrew Barnes, *St. Petersburg Times*; Philip Baur, Jr., Tasty Baking Company; Ron Blue, Ron Blue & Company; Frank Brock, formerly of Brock Candy Co., currently with Covenant College; Bob Buford, Buford Television, Inc.; Bill Burnson, Eckerd pharmacist; Truett Cathy, Chick-fil-A; Tom Chappell, Tom's of Maine; Max DePree, Herman Miller, Inc.; C. Fred Fetterolf, formerly with Alcoa Aluminum; Barbara Hammond, Home Interiors & Gifts; James Henderson, Cummins Engine; Terry Hershberger, Security Group, Inc.; Rick Hyatt, The Home Depot; David T. Kearns, former CEO of Xerox, currently Deputy Secretary of Education; Alonzo "Al" McDonald, Avenir Group; Gustavo Mir, Chick-fil-A; Hugh Morton, Jr., North Carolina; Ed Noble, Noble Properties; Peter Ochs, The Fieldstone Company; Byron Oliver, CIGNA; Ross Perot, The Perot Group; Henry J. "Bud" Smith, Clark/Bardes, Inc.; Phil Stalas, Jack Eckerd Corp.; Tom Van Dyk, Herman Miller, Inc.; Bill Watkins, Associates Industries; and Kenneth Wessner, ServiceMaster, Inc.

We used many insights drawn from these interviews in two ways. First, quotations were taken directly from some of the interviews. Also, we took some literary license by incorporating quotes from interviews into anecdotal stories that reflect typical business exchanges. In some cases we used fictional names for individuals appearing in the stories. Our desire was to enhance the impact and meaning of some of the most significant observations expressed during the interviews.

A word of thanks is also in order to those who read, reviewed, and critiqued the manuscript. As always, Carl F. H. Henry, although one of the busiest men we know, and clearly one of America's foremost theologians, was the first to respond with his wonderfully helpful and insightful suggestions; Os Guinness, a great thinker and a real authority on the subject of vocation and calling, was equally helpful; as was Chuck's old friend and one-time colleague, Herb Stein, former chairman of the President's Council on Economic Advisors. Thanks also to Doug Bandow of the Cato

Institute; to Kurt Schaefer, professor of economics at Calvin College; to Ron Nash, who until recently was chairman of the department of philosophy at Western Kentucky University, and now is on faculty at Reformed Theological Seminary; and to Ed Feulner of the Heritage Foundation.

Finally, we give thanks for the great privilege of working together on this book. We come from two distinct points of view, and each of us tried to balance his experience—Jack's in business and government, and Chuck's in government and ministry—to meet the wide range of experiences and beliefs of our readers. Hopefully others will realize, as we do, the gravity of the crisis in our country and join us in working for effective change.

There are bound to be some dicey moments when two hardheaded, strong-willed individuals team up, but we found it to be a joyful experience that has cemented our friendship even more firmly. And we're profoundly and eternally grateful to the One who changed our lives, brought us together, and uses us, we pray even now, as instruments in the working out of His sovereign will.

Charles Colson
Jack Eckerd
August 1, 1991

Notes

Introduction

1. The concentration camp story was originally told, in slightly different form, in Charles Colson, *Kingdoms in Conflict* (Grand Rapids, Mich.: William Morrow and Zondervan Publishing House, 1987), 67, 68; see also Eugene Heimler, *Mental Illness*, a study quoted in Joseph Frank, *Dostoevsky: Years of Ordeal* (Princeton, N.J.: Princeton University Press, 1983), 159.

Chapter 1 • *Something's Not Working*

1. Bill Moyers, *A World of Ideas* (New York: Doubleday, 1990), 408.
2. Aleksandr Solzhenitsyn, "How to Revitalize Russia," quoted in *New York Times*, 18 September 1990.
3. Ronald Dawkins, "'91 Caprice Police Cruisers Spinning Their Wheel Covers," *Miami Herald*, 13 July 1991.
4. Findings of the Council on Competitiveness, cited by David S. Broder, "Americans Showing Concern at Home," *Miami Herald*, 15 July 1991.
5. Lance Morrow, "What Is the Point of Working?" *Time*, 11 May 1981, 93.

6. Anna Quindlen, "Preventive Medicine," *New York Times*, 25 April 1991, editorial page.

7. The March 1990 delegation was headed by Michael Quinlan, Director, Federal Bureau of Prisons, United States Department of Justice.

8. For data on Soviet conditions, see, Richard Hornik, "Winter's Bitter Wind," *Time*, 4 December 1989; Jane Kramer, "Letter from Europe," *New Yorker*, 12 March 1990; and Robert Conquest, "Back to the USSR," *National Review*, 18 August 1989.

Chapter 2 • We're Number Five

1. Lance Morrow, "What Is the Point of Working?" *Time*, 11 May 1981, 93.

2. "Only One Domestic Automaker Division Rated Among Top Five," UPI, 9 June 1990.

3. "Lexus Infiniti Tops in Owner Satisfaction," Associated Press, 9 July 1991.

4. David Woodruff, "A New Era for Auto Quality," *Business Week*, 22 October 1990, 84.

5. *Wilson Quarterly* (Autumn 1990): 75.

6. David E. Singer, "When the Corporate Lab Goes to Japan," *New York Times*, 28 April 1991, 3:1.

7. "Japan's Business Acumen World's Best Study Says," Reuters News Service, *Miami Herald*, 20 June 1991, 2C.

8. Ross Perot, interview with Jack Eckerd, May 1991.

9. *America's Choice: High Skills or Low Wages: The Report of the Commission on the Skills of the American Workforce*, National Center on Education and the Economy, June 1990, 8. The commission preparing this report was chaired by Ira Magaziner and co-chaired by Bill Brock and Ray Marshall. Since this report has been known as "the Brock report" in the press, and for the sake of brevity, we have used that term later in referring to it.

10. Ibid., 21.

11. David Broder, "Bush Rating Masks Underlying Pessimism," *Chicago Tribune*, 14 July 1991, 3C.

12. James Simmons, *Americans: The View from Abroad* (New York: Harmony Books, 1990), 167.

13. *America's Choice*, 57.

14. Phil Gailey, "CEO's Salaries: Up, Up and Away," *St. Petersburg Times*, 17 June 1991.

15. Ibid. Also, Communications Office, Association of Flight Attendants, AFL-CIO, 30 July 1991.

16. "Postal Service Gatherings at Plush Resorts Receive Stamp of Disapproval," Knight-Ridder News Service, 16 March 1990.

17. Ed Blazina and Janet Williams, "Postal Brasses Reap Bonuses," *Washington Times*, 5 July 1991.

18. Philip H. Mirvis and Donald L. Kanter, "Combatting Cynicism in the Workplace," *National Productivity Review*, vol. 8, no. 4 (Autumn 1989): 379.

19. Associated Press, "Survey Finds Office Workers Less Satisfied with Jobs," 31 March 1989.

20. Gisela Bolte, "Will Americans Work for $5 a Day?" *Time*, 23 July 1990, 12.

21. Frank Swoboda, "Union Leader: Managers Pull the Strings in 'Team' Programs," *Washington Post*, 14 April 1991.

22. Daniel Yankelovitch, "The New Psychological Contracts at Work," *Psychology Today*, May 1978, 49–50.

23. Dana Priest, "Postal Workers 'Nonproductive' Time Said to Triple in 20 Years," *Washington Post*, 21 September 1990.

24. Daniel Yankelovitch, "The Work Ethic Is Underemployed," *Psychology Today*, May 1982, 5.

25. Arthur Burns, 1977 commencement address, University of South Carolina.

26. Doug Sherman and William Hendricks, *Your Work Matters to God* (Colorado Springs: NavPress, 1987).

Chapter 3 • The Roots of Work

1. Morrow, "What Is the Point of Working?"

2. Pope John Paul II, *Laborem Exercens* (On Human Work) (Washington, D.C.: United States Catholic Conference, 1981), 1.

3. *Calvin's New Testament Commentaries* (Grand Rapids, Mich.: Eerdmans, 1972), 88.

4. God assigned Adam and Eve their tasks before the curse, not after; work itself is not a result of a cosmic curse. This is a crucial point, the misunderstanding of which has caused grave confusion and distorted

the view of work from a biblical perspective. Even one as perceptive as Lance Morrow missed it when he wrote: "When God foreclosed on Eden, He condemned Adam and Eve to go to work. Work has never recovered from that humiliation . . . from the beginning the Lord's Word said that work was something bad; a punishment, the great stone of mortality and toil laid upon the human spirit that might otherwise soar in the infinite weightless, playfulness of grace" (Morrow, "What Is the Point of Working?").

5. Exodus 20:8–11, 15, 17.

6. William Barclay, *Ethics in a Permissive Society* (New York: Harper & Row, 1971), 94.

7. Ecclesiastes 5:18–19.

8. Adriano Tigler, *Homo Faber: Work Through the Ages* (Chicago: Henry Regnery and Co., 1965), 3.

9. 2 Thessalonians 3:10.

10. Kenneth Scott Latourette, *A History of Christianity* (New York: Harper & Row, 1953), 246.

11. Martin Luther, *The Babylonian Captivity*, as quoted by Os Guinness in his speech "Ordering Our Calling In and To the World."

12. David Vogel, "Business Ethics Past and Present," *The Public Interest* (Winter 1991): 49–64.

13. Quoted in George Grant, *Bringing in the Sheaves: Transforming Poverty into Productivity* (Atlanta: American Vision, 1985), 76.

14. Christians in both the Catholic and Protestant traditions today vigorously defend the view of democratic capitalism that emerged from the Reformation. The most recent and eloquent example is Pope John Paul II's encyclical of May 1991 defending the free market and private profit. While the differences between Catholic and Protestant views of work have been greatly modified in recent years, we should note one continuing difference. Formal Catholic doctrine makes a distinction between the priest, who is ordained to holy office as a successor of the apostles, and other workers, who are not part of the priesthood. Workers are not priests, but neither are priests workers. For a more thorough treatment of this point, see Carl F. H. Henry, "The Christian View of Work," in *Aspects of Christian Social Ethics* (Grand Rapids, Mich.: Eerdmans, 1964).

15. The reason we say this is that while the work ethic was developed through centuries of Christian tradition, the high view of work comes from the Creation covenant, which precedes both the Jewish and Christian traditions and which has universal application for all mankind.

16. David T. Rodgers, *The Work Ethic in Industrial America* (Chicago: University of Chicago Press, 1978), 4.

17. Leland Ryken, *Worldly Saints: The Puritans as They Really Were* (Grand Rapids, Mich.: Zondervan Publishing House, 1986), 27.

18. Ibid., 31.

19. Morrow, "What Is the Point of Working?"

20. Sherwood Wirt, "A Study of the Relation of the Christian (Post-Reformation) Concept of Vocation to the Modern Development of State-Controlled Vocational Guidance," Ph.D. diss., University of Edinburgh, 1951.

21. Os Guinness, "Ordering Our Calling in and to the World."

Chapter 4 • The Revolution

1. Nicola Chiaromonte, "Albert Camus: In Memoriam," from *Camus: A Collection of Critical Essays,* ed. Germaine Bree (Englewood Cliffs, N.J.: Prentice-Hall, 1962), 14.

2. *James Weinstein, Studies on the Left: RIP, Radical America* (vol. 1, no. 3 , 1967), 3.

3. Ibid, 1, 2.

4. Martin Nicolaus, "The Contradiction of Advanced Capitalist Society and Its Resolution," cited in Joe Ferrandino, "Rock Culture and the Development of Social Conscience," *Radical American,* vol. 3, no. 6, 1969.

5. Studs Terkel, *Working* (New York: Pantheon, 1974), xi.

Chapter 5 • The Society That Preys Together

1. Bill Moyers, *A World of Ideas* (New York: Doubleday, 1990), 66.

2. Daniel Yankelovitch, "The New Psychological Contracts at Work," *Psychology Today,* May 1978, 49–50.

3. *Washington Times,* 20 May 1991.

4. George Watson, "The Decay of Idleness," *Wilson Quarterly* (Spring 1991): 110.

5. Tad Friend, "Michael Milken Free at Last!" *Esquire,* May 1991, 74–86.

6. Ronald Henkoff, "Is Greed Dead?" *Fortune*, 14 August 1989, 40.

7. Tom Wolfe, *Bonfire of the Vanities* (New York: Bantam Books, 1988), 234–40.

8. Russell P. Boisjoly and Ellen Foster Curtis, "Roger Boisjoly and the Challenger Disaster: A Case Study in Management Practice, Corporate Loyalty and Business Ethics," in W. Michael Hoffman, *Business Ethics: Readings and Cases* (New York: McGraw Hill, 1990), 397.

9. Ibid.

10. T. Bancroft, "Two Minutes," *Financial World*, 27 June 1989, 28–29.

11. "Bad Apples: In the Executive Suite, *Consumer Reports*, May 1989, 294.

12. Daniel Yankelovitch, "The Work Ethic Is Underemployed," *Psychology Today*, May 1982, 5.

13. Robert Bellah, *Habits of the Heart* (New York: Harper & Row, 1985).

14. James Sheehy, "New Work Ethic Is Frightening," *Personnel Journal*, June 1990, 28–36.

Chapter 6 • A Nation at Risk

1. Richard Mitchell, *Less Than Words Can Say* (Boston: Little, Brown, 1979), 79.

2. Diane Ravitch and Chester Finn, *What Do Our 17-Year-Olds Know?* (New York: Harper & Row, 1987), 43–120.

3. "Harper's Index," *Harper's*, October 1990, 17.

4. "U.S. Scores Dead Last in Math Among 6 Nations' 13-Year-Olds," *San Francisco Chronicle*, 1 February 1989, as cited in Claremont Institute's Golden State Briefings, 1:2.

5. Lawrence A. Uzzell, "Education Reform Fails the Test," *Wall Street Journal*, 10 May 1989, as cited in Claremont Institute's Golden State Briefings, 1:3.

6. "Sweaty Palms, Circa 1914," *Wall Street Journal*, 31 March 1989, as cited in Claremont Institute's Golden State Briefings, 1:3.

7. Uzzell, "Education Reform."

8. *A Nation at Risk*, National Commission on Excellence in Education, 1983, 5.

9. See Paul C. Vitz, *Censorship: Evidence of Bias in Our Children's Textbooks* (Ann Arbor, Mich.: Servant Books, 1986).

10. "Adolescent Stages of Growth: Critical Events and Characteris-

tic Behaviors," *Teacher's Resource Guide: Adolescence and Adulthood*, Fairfax County Public Schools, Fairfax, Virginia, AA-1.

11. Bill Honig, *Last Chance for Our Children* (Reading, Mass.: Addison-Wesley, 1985), 94.

12. Ibid., 151.

13. Richard Cohen, "Self-Esteem: Sorry, No Extra Credit," *Washington Post*, 12 June 1991.

14. Lynn V. Cheney, *American Memory* (Washington, D.C.: National Endowment for the Humanities, 1987), 25, as cited in Claremont Institute's Golden State Briefings, 2:3.

15. Steven Hayward, "Bill Honig's Reform Movement Seems Largely a Fraud," *San Diego Union*, 29 May 1987.

16. Dana Wechsler, "Parkinson's Law 101," *Forbes*, 25 June 1990.

17. Don Feder, "American Education Reform Is Gigantic Fraud," *Sacramento Union*, 13 September 1987.

18. "Education Stagnated in the U.S. Cavazo Says," *San Diego Union*, 4 May 1989.

19. Paul Copperman, *The Literacy Hoax: The Decline of Reading, Writing, and Learning in the Public Schools and What We Can Do About It* (New York: Morrow, 1978), 15.

20. Chester E. Finn, Jr., "A Nation Still at Risk," *Commentary* (May 1989), 17.

21. John E. Chubb and Terry M. Moe, *Politics, Markets, and America's Schools* (Washington, D.C.: Brookings Institute, 1990), 9.

22. *America's Choice*, 121.

Chapter 7 • *A Generation Condemned*

1. Jack Kemp, "How We Trap America's Poor in the 'Other Economy,'" *Washington Post*, 26 May 1991, D1. Kemp is secretary of housing and urban development.

2. George Will, "Lessons of Cabrini Green," *Washington Post*, 30 March 1989, A23.

3. James Gwartney, "Have Antipoverty Programs Increased Poverty?" *Cato Journal*, vol. 5, no. 1 (Spring-Summer 1985): 1–16.

4. Marvin Olasky, "Beyond the Stingy Welfare State: What We Can Learn from the Compassion of the 19th Cenutry," *Policy Review* (Fall 1990): 2.

5. William Julius Wilson, *The Truly Disadvantaged: The Inner City, the Underclass, and Public Policy* (Chicago: University of Chicago Press, 1987), 65.

6. William Tucker, "Our Homestead Plan for the Poor," *American Spectator*, July 1988, 26.

7. Myron Magnet, "America's Underclass: What to Do?" *Fortune*, 11 May 1987, 132.

8. Eugene H. Methvin, "How Uncle Sam Robbed America's Poor," *Reader's Digest* (April 1985), 136.

9. George Gilder, "Welfare Spurs Family Breakdown," *Insight*, 23 May 1986.

10. Valerie Gladstone, "The Unsinkable Katie Brown," *Tropic*, 16 September 1990, 17.

11. Gwartney, "Have Antipoverty Programs Increased Poverty?"

Chapter 8 • *Transforming the Culture*

1. Robert Coles, "The Moral Life of the Young," Address to the American Society of Newspaper Editors, Cambridge, Mass., 10 April 1991.

2. President Bush's 1991 nominee for Supreme Court Justice, quoted in William Raspberry, "Judge Thomas: Up Close and Personal," *Miami Herald*, 5 July 1991, 13A.

3. Ralph Z. Hollow, "Wilder: Black Teens Need Stronger Values," *Washington Times*, 16 April 1991.

4. William Raspberry, "Rights and Outcomes, Remedies and Goals," *Washington Post*, 22 March 1991.

5. William Raspberry, "What Manner of Man, Clarence Thomas?" *Washington Post*, 3 July 1991, A19.

6. Fred Gosman, *Spoiled Rotten—American Children and How to Change Them* (Milwaukee: Bashford and O'Neill, 1990), quoted in Kim Conyer, "Spoiled Rotten," *Miami Herald*, 17 February 1991, 1F.

7. James Wilson and Richard Herrnstein, *Crime and Human Nature* (New York: Simon and Schuster, 1985).

Chapter 9 • *To the Heart: A Moral Education*

1. George F. Will, "A Moral Environment for the Poor," *Washington Post*, 30 May 1991, A19. Will also notes that in Wesley's day

"industrialism was uprooting villagers, sucking them into cities where many succumbed to a new form of an old drug—gin. It was as devastating as crack has been. London had 17,000 gin shops. . . . Wesley, who tirelessly [250,000 miles] rode Britain's rural roads and city streets, evangelized the underclass, exhorting pride and combating family disintegration by reforming behavior."

2. Dorothy Sayers, *Creed or Chaos* (New York: Harcourt Brace, 1949), 56.

3. Ibid.

4. John Alexander, "Capitalism Reconsidered," *Taking Jesus Seriously*, vol. 3, no. 1, January-February 1987, 2.

5. Robert Tilton, *God's Miracle Plan for Man* (Dallas: Robert Tilton Ministries, 1987).

6. See Pope John Paul II, *Laborem Exercens*.

7. Carl F. H. Henry, *Aspects of Christian Social Ethics* (Grand Rapids, Mich.: Eerdmans, 1964), 40.

8. See Pope John Paul II, *Laborem Exercens*, sec. 6.

9. R. C. Sproul, *Ethics and the Christian* (Wheaton, Ill.: Tyndale House, 1983), 60.

10. Mark Dawidziak, "Lear Mixes Religion into 'Sunday Dinner,'" *San Diego Union*, 29 January 1991.

11. Will, "A Moral Environment."

12. Garth Wood, *The Myth of Neurosis: Overcoming the Illness Excuse* (New York: Harper & Row, 1983).

13. Ibid.

14. Derek Bok, "Ethics, the University, and Society," *Harvard Magazine* (May-June 1988): 39.

15. Margo Hammond, "Tom Wolfe Delivers a Label for the Decade," *St. Petersburg Times*, 27 March 1991, 3B.

16. "Good Morning America," 25 July 1991.

Chapter 10 • Back to Basics

1. Excerpt of "A Nation at Risk," *The American Reader*, ed. Diane Ravitch (New York: Harper Collins Publishers, 1990), 361–62.

2. "Teachers vs. Kids," *Wall Street Journal*, 6 June 1990.

3. "Blocking the Schoolhouse Door," *Wall Street Journal*, 27 June 1990.

4. Honig, *Last Chance for Our Children*, 92.

5. John E. Chubb and Terry Moe, *Politics, Markets and America's Schools* (Washington, D.C.: Brookings Institute, 1990), 3.

6. William Raspberry, "The Public Schools' Bad Work Habits," *Washington Post,* 1 October 1990.

7. Quoted in Richard Mitchell, *The Graves of Academe* (Boston: Little, Brown, 1981), 159.

8. Raymond English, interview, April 1989.

9. "Oregon Begins Bold Plan to Reshape Education," *Miami Herald,* 18 July 1991, 19A.

Chapter 11 • Freeing the Slaves

1. Valerie Gladstone, "The Unsinkable Katie Brown," *Tropic,* 16 September 1990.

2. Spencer Rich, "Sullivan's Sermon: Responsibility," *Washington Post,* 19 March 1991.

3. Marlise Simons, "The Dutch Forget the Work Ethic and Call in Sick," *New York Times,* 6 October 1990.

4. John Paul II, *Centesimus Annus,* 1991, sec. 48.

5. "A New Child Support Assurance System," Institute for Research on Poverty, U.S. Department of Health and Human Services. Paper #916–90.

6. Marvin Olasky, "Beyond the Stingy Welfare State: What We Can Learn from the Compassion of the 19th Century," *Policy Review* (Fall 1990): 2.

7. Nicholas Davidson, "Life Without Father," *Policy Review* (Winter 1990).

8. David C. Anderson, *Crimes of Justice: Improving the Police, the Courts, the Prisons* (New York: Time Books, 1988), 274–76.

9. Glenn D. Walters and Thomas W. White, "Society and Lifestyle Criminality," *Federal Probation* (December 1988).

10. Waldemar Nielsen, *Some Lessons from One Effort at Prison Reform,* Chronicles of Philanthrophy, 7 May 1991.

11. State of Florida, Office of the Auditor General, Report no. 11594, Performance Audit of the Prison Industries Program Administered by Prison Rehabilitation Industries and Diversified Enterprises, Inc., 4 March 1991.

12. Warren E. Burger, "Ex-prisoners Can Become Producers, Not

Predators," *Nation's Business,* October 1983, 38–39.

13. Barbara J. Auerbach et al., *Work in American Prisons: The Private Sector Gets Involved* (Washington, D.C.: National Institute of Justice, 1988), 28.

14. Michael Isikoff, "Does Inmate Labor Work?" *Washington Post,* 12 November 1990.

15. Elmer H. Johnson, *Open Prisons in the Japanese Manner,* Center for the Study of Crime, Delinquency, and Corrections (Carbondale: Southern Illinois University), 15–18.

16. Jack Eckerd interviews, May 1989.

17. John Boal, "Helping Prison Work," *American Way,* January 1986.

18. Michael Isikoff, "Does Inmate Labor Work?" *Washington Post,* November 12, 1990.

19. Barbara J. Auerbach et al., *Work in American Prisons: The Private Sector Gets Involved* (Washington, D.C.: National Institute of Justice, 1988), 26.

20. David Glidden, "Put Inmates to Work, Make Prison Produce," *Los Angeles Times,* 1 April 1990.

Chapter 12 • Restoring the Marketplace

1. Perry Pascarella, *The New Achievers: Creating a Modern Work Ethic* (New York: Free Press, 1984), 24–25.

2. James Henderson, interview with Jack Eckerd, 13 March 1991.

3. Fred Fetterolf, interview with Jack Eckerd, 25 April 1991. Also see Laura Sessions Steep, "In Search of Ethics," *Washington Post,* 31 March 1991.

4. Jack Reichert, "America Leadership and Values in the '90s," speech to the graduating class of Carroll College, Waukesha, Wis., 19 May 1991.

5. Peter Ochs, interview with Jack Eckerd, 7 March 1991.

6. Max DePree, *Leadership Is an Art* (East Lansing: Michigan State University Press, 1987).

7. Ibid.

8. Kay Collier-Stone, "Everyday Ethics for Christ's Sake," *The Advocate of the Episcopal Diocese of Lexington, Kentucky,* April 1991, 7.

9. Terry Hershberger, interview with Jim Roberts, 7 June 1991.

10. R. C. Sproul, *Stronger Than Steel: The Wayne Alderson Story* (New York: Harper & Row, 1980).

11. Ibid.

12. Ibid.

13. Wayne Alderson, telephone interview with Laura Grace Alexander, 8 July 1991.

14. Frank Brock, interview with Jack Eckerd, 24 January 1991.

15. DePree, *Leadership Is an Art.*

16. Nancy Gladstone, "Don't Mess with Success," *Washington Post National Weekly Edition,* August-September 1990.

17. James Henderson, interview with Jack Eckerd, 13 March 1991. See also speech, Henderson presentation to Rohm and Haas Management Group, 14 February 1991.

18. Tom Van Dyk, interview with Jim Roberts, 18 April 1991.

19. Bob Buford, interview with Jim Roberts, 9 April 1991.

20. Peter Ochs, interview with Jack Eckerd, 7 March 1991.

21. Ross Perot, interview with Jack Eckerd, 8 April 1991.

22. Fred Fetterolf, interview with Jack Eckerd, 25 April 1991.

23. Frank Brock, interview with Jack Eckerd, 24 January 1991.

24. Robin Luymes, "Quiet Giant: Prince Corporation Emerges," *Grand Rapids Business Journal,* 15 July 1991.

25. Bob Buford, interview with Jim Roberts, 9 April 1991.

26. Barbara Hammond, interview with Jack Eckerd, 22 May 1991.

27. Ken Wessner, interview with Jack Eckerd, 26 January 1991. Also see Wessner's chapter in *What My Parents Did Right,* comp., Gloria Gaither.

28. Philip Baur, interview with Jack Eckerd, 20 March 1991.

29. Luymes, "Quiet Giant."

30. Gustavo Mir, interview with Jim Roberts, April 1991.

31. Ken Wessner, interview with Jack Eckerd, 26 January 1991.

32. David Kearns, interview with Jack Eckerd, 6 June 1991. Kearns is current deputy secretary of education, U.S. Department of Education.

33. Bill Burnson, interview with Jim Roberts, 17 April 1991.

34. David Kearns, interview with Jack Eckerd, 6 June 1991.

35. Ross Perot, interview with Jack Eckerd, 8 April 1991.

36. Ed Noble, interview with Jack Eckerd, 22 April 1991.

37. Fred Fetterolf, interview with Jack Eckerd, 25 April 1991.

38. Philip Baur, interview with Jack Eckerd, 20 March 1991.

39. Ross Perot, interview with Jack Eckerd, 8 April 1991.

40. Byron Oliver, interview with Jack Eckerd, 15 April 1991. Also, Frank Beneski and Douglas Van Ryn, interviews with Jim Roberts, May–June 1991.

41. Andrew Barnes, interview with Jack Eckerd, 13 May 1991.

42. Frank Brock, interview with Jack Eckerd, 24 January 1991.

43. Bryon Oliver, interview with Jack Eckerd, 15 April 1991.

Conclusion

1. Retold from a story told by John Stott.

Further Reading

For those who want a more in-depth study of the issues raised in this book, we have compiled a brief reading list. Readers may find some of these useful.

Alison, Michael. *Christianity and Conservatism*. London: Hodder & Stoughton, 1990.

———. "World Poverty and Christian Responsibility." Unpublished paper.

Baldwin, Stanley C. *Take This Job and Love It*. Downers Grove, Ill.: InterVarsity Press, 1988.

Bane, Mary Jo, and David T. Ellwood. "The Dynamics of Dependence: The Routes to Self-Sufficiency." Report prepared for U.S. Department of Health and Human Services. June 1983.

Beisner, E. Calvin. *Prosperity and Poverty: The Compassionate Use of Resources in a World of Scarcity*. Westchester, Ill.: Crossway Books, 1988.

Berger, Peter L. "Some General Observations on the Problem of Work." In *The Human Shape of Work. Studies in the Sociology of*

Occupations, 211–14. New York and London: Collier and Macmillan, 1964.

Bernbaum, John A., and Simon Steer. *Why Work? Careers and Employment in Biblical Perspective*. Grand Rapids: Baker Book House, 1987.

Bernstein, P. "The Work Ethic: Economics, Not Religion." *Business Horizons* (May-June 1988): 8–11.

Bieler, Andre. *The Social Humanism of Calvin*. Translated by P. T. Fuhrmann. Richmond: John Knox Press, 1964.

Browning, Edgar. *Redistribution and the Welfare System*. Washington, D.C.: American Enterprise Institute, 1975.

Butler, Stuart, and Anna Kondratas. *Out of the Poverty Trap*. New York: The Free Press, 1987.

Catherwood, Henry F. R. *The Christian in Industrial Society*. London: Tyndale, 1966.

———. *God's Time, God's Money*. London: Hodder & Stoughton, 1987.

———. *On the Job: The Christian 9 to 5*. Grand Rapids, Mich.: Zondervan Publishing House, 1980.

Chan, Warren. "A Return to the Work Ethic." *Judges Journal* 27 (Winter 1988): 29, 38.

Chewning, Richard C., ed. *Biblical Principles and Economics: The Foundations*. Colorado Springs: NavPress, 1989.

Davis, John Jefferson. *Your Wealth in God's World*. Phillipsburg, N.J.: Presbyterian and Reformed Publishing House, 1984.

de Soto, Hernando. *The Other Path: The Invisible Revolution in the Third World*. New York: Harper & Row, 1989.

DePree, Max. *Leadership Is an Art*. New York: Doubleday, 1989.

Diehl, William. *In Search of Faithfulness*. Minneapolis: Augsburg/Fortress Press, 1987.

———. *Thank God It's Monday*. Minneapolis: Augsburg/Fortress Press, 1982.

Douglas, Jack D. *The Myth of the Welfare State.* New Brunswick, N.J.: Transaction, 1989.

Drucker, Peter F. *The Age of Discontinuity.* New York: Harper & Row, 1969.

————. *The Art of Leadership.* New York: Doubleday, 1989.

Engstrom, Ted W., and David J. Juroe. *The Work Trap.* Old Tappan, N.J.: Fleming H. Revell, 1979.

Field, David, and Elspheth Stepheson. *Just the Job: Christians Talk about Work and Vocation.* Leicester: InterVarsity, 1978.

Grant, George. *Bringing in the Sheaves: Transforming Poverty into Productivity.* Brentwood, Tenn.: Wolgemuth and Hyatt, 1988.

Griffiths, Brian. *The Creation of Wealth.* Leicester: InterVarsity, 1989.

Guinness, Os. *Winning Back the Soul of American Business.* Burke, Va.: Hourglass, 1990.

Gwartney, J., and T. S. McCaleb. "Have Antipoverty Programs Increased Poverty?" *Cato Journal* 5 (Spring-Summer 1985): 1–16.

Hardy, Lee. *The Fabric of This World.* Grand Rapids, Mich.: Eerdmans, 1990.

Hatch, Nathan O., ed. *The Professions in American History.* South Bend, Ind.: University of Notre Dame Press, 1988.

Henry, Carl F. H. "The Christian View of Work." In *Aspects of Christian Social Ethics,* 31–71. Grand Rapids, Mich.: Eerdmans, 1964.

Hybels, Bill. *Christians in the Marketplace.* Wheaton, Ill.: Victor Books, 1986.

Hyde, Henry J. "Is the Market Moral?" *National Review,* 5 November 1990, 52–54.

Johnson, Paul. "The Capitalism and Morality Debate." *First Things* (March 1990): 18–22.

Kaus, Mickey, "The Work Ethic State: The Only Way to Break the Culture of Poverty." *New Republic,* 7 July 1986, 22–33.

Kendall, G. A. "Bureaucracy and Welfare: The Enslavement of the Spirit." *Social Justice Review* (May-June 1990): 104–7.

Liebig, James. *Business Ethics: Profiles in Civic Virtue*. Golden, Colo.: Fulcrum, 1990.

Mahedy, William, and C. Carstens. *Starting on Monday: Christian Living in the Workplace*. New York: Ballantine, 1987.

Martino, Antonio. "Statism at Work: The Italian Case." In *Champions of Freedom*, edited by R. L. Trowbridge, 15–35. Ludwig von Mises Lecture Series, no. 8. Hillsdale, Mich.: Hillsdale College, 1981.

Mattox, Robert. *The Christian Employee*. Plainfield, N.J.: Logos International, 1978.

Mattson, Ralph, and Arthur Miller. *Finding a Job You Can Love*. Nashville: Thomas Nelson, 1982.

McKenna, David L. *Love Your Work*. Wheaton, Ill.: Victor Books, 1990.

Mead, Lawrence M. "Jobs for the Welfare Poor: Work Requirements Can Overcome the Barriers." *Policy Review* 43 (Winter 1988): 60–69.

———. "The New Politics of the New Poverty." *Public Interest* 103 (Spring 1991): 3–20.

Methvin, E. H. "How Uncle Sam Robbed America's Poor." *Reader's Digest* (April 1985): 135–44.

Middelmann, Udo. *Pre-Existence*. Downers Grove, Ill.: InterVarsity Press, 1974.

Murray, Charles. *Losing Ground: American Social Policy*, 1950–1980. New York: Basic Books, 1984.

Nash, Ronald H. *Freedom, Justice and the State*. Lanham, Md.: University Press of America, 1980.

———. *Poverty and Wealth: The Christian Debate over Capitalism*. Westchester, Ill.: Crossway Books, 1986.

Neuhaus, Richard John. "Wealth and Whimsy: On Economic Creativity." *First Things* (August-September 1990): 23–30.

Novak, Michael. *The Spirit of Democratic Capitalism*. New York: Simon & Schuster, 1982.

———. *Toward a Theology of the Corporation.* Washington, D.C., and London: American Enterprise Institute, 1981.

Olasky, Marvin. "Beyond the Stingy Welfare State." *Policy Review* 54 (Fall 1990): 2–14.

Peabody, Larry. *Secular Work Is Full-Time Service.* Fort Washington, Pa.: Christian Literature Crusade, 1974.

Peters, Thomas J. *In Search of Excellence.* New York: Harper & Row, 1982.

Pope John Paul II. "Centesimus Annus (The 100th Year)." *Origins* 21/1, 16 May 1991, 1–23.

———. "Laborem Exercens (On Human Work)." *Origins* 11/15, 14 September 1981, 225–45.

Read, Leonard E. "The Something-for-Nothing Syndrome." In *Champions of Freedom,* edited by S. F. Briggs, 23–35. Ludwig von Mises Lecture Series, no. 4. Hillsdale, Mich.: Hillsdale College, 1977.

Roche, George. "Morality in the Marketplace." In *One by One: Preserving Values and Freedom in Heartland America,* 125–38. Hillsdale, Mich.: Hillsdale College, 1990.

Rodgers, Daniel T. *The Work Ethic in Industrial America.* Chicago: University of Chicago Press, 1978.

Ryken, Leland. "Puritan Work Ethic: The Dignity of Life's Labors." *Christianity Today,* 19 October 1979, 14–19.

———. *Worldly Saints: The Puritans as They Really Were.* Grand Rapids, Mich.: Zondervan Publishing House, 1986.

Sayers, Dorothy L. *Why Work?* London: Methuen & Co., 1942.

Schlossberg, Herbert. "Idols of Mammon." In *Idols for Destruction,* 88–139. Nashville: Thomas Nelson, 1983.

Sowell, Thomas. *Markets and Minorities.* New York: Basic Books, 1981.

Schumacher, E. F. *Economic Development and Poverty.* London: Africa Bureau, 1966.

———. *Good Work.* New York: Harper & Row, 1979.

————. *Roots of Economic Growth.* Varanasi: Gandhian Institute of Studies, 1961.

Schwartz, Joel. "The Moral Environment of the Poor." *Public Interest* 103 (Spring 1991): 21–37.

Sherman, Doug, and William Hendricks. *Your Work Matters to God.* Colorado Springs: NavPress, 1987.

Sproul, R. C. *Stronger than Steel.* New York: Harper & Row, 1980.

Steele, Richard. *The Trademan's Calling.* Hartford, Conn.: Mills Printers, 1903.

White, Jerry, and Mary White. *Your Job—Survival or Satisfaction?* Grand Rapids, Mich.: Zondervan Publishing House, 1977.

Our thanks to Pete Hammond for his assistance in compiling this list. For a more extensive reading list on this topic, contact Pete Hammond at Market Place, 6400 Schroeder Road, P. O. Box 7895, Madison, Wis. 53707-7895.

Index